Open to All

"I have always imagined that Paradise will be a kind of library."
— Jorge Louis Borges

Whenever the shelves of the Library of Heaven were entirely full, and a new worthy book appeared, all the books in the celestial collection pressed themselves closer together and made room.
— a Talmudic legend

"What is more important in a library than anything else—than everything else—is the fact that it exists."
— Archibald MacLeish

"Libraries are reservoirs of strength, grace, and wit, reminders of order, calm, and continuity, lakes of mental energy, neither warm nor cold, light nor dark. The pleasure they give is steady, reliable, deep and long-lasting. In any library in the world, I am at home, unselfconscious, still and absorbed."
— Germaine Greer

What the Library Means to Me

AN ANTHOLOGY

Edited by

Molly Fisk, Steve Fjeldsted & Steve Sanfield

COMSTOCK BONANZA PRESS
GRASS VALLEY CALIFORNIA

Published in 2007 by Comstock Bonanza Press
18919 William Quirk Memorial Drive
Grass Valley, CA 95945-8611
for the Nevada County Library
and the Nevada County Library Foundation

LIMITED FIRST EDITION

COPYRIGHT NOTICE:

Each contribution to this book is the sole property
of its author or creator and is protected by
individual copyright. Permission to reprint
any work contained herein must be obtained
in writing from the author or creator of that work.

ISBN 978-0-933994-35-5

This anthology is dedicated to Elaine May Channel
January 1, 1928 – January 7, 2006

Elaine was a member of the Friends of the Library Board of Directors. In her quiet and unassuming way she was a fierce supporter of the Library. As Tom Dunham said at her memorial service: "During the last four years I asked Elaine's advice nearly every week. The newspaper notice said she had a keen, analytical mind. I think that is a gross understatement. In addition to being very bright and unusually good with numbers she was also very practical and sensible. She could simplify the most complex problems to the essentials. And, she always told me when I was wrong in the nicest way possible. Thanks, Elaine, for everything."

Introductions

ONE of the things I love in this world is evidence of democracy, and the American Public Library embodies this more than anything I know. There are no age restrictions. The color of your skin doesn't keep you out. Men and women don't have separate doors. Borrowing books is free unless you keep them overtime and maybe, after the one-week grace period, have to pay a really minuscule fine. There are usually bathrooms, a water fountain, often some front steps you can sit on to wait for your mom to pick you up. It's warm there in the winter, and cool in the summer, and open to all. It's fabulous.

When Steve Fjeldsted and I were brainstorming about ways to raise money to buy more books for the library, I thought of how moved I'd been by a friend's account of going to the library with her mother—a generally chilly mother, who unbent and became generous at the library, thereby fostering her daughter's love of language and writing. I wanted to know who else had stories like this, of transformation and salvation, as well as of pleasure and self-discovery.

So we embarked on this book, me and the two Steves, and we hope you like it. Of course we want you to buy it, in order to raise book-buying funds, but if you can't, or won't, or aren't sure yet, you can always check it out of the library.

— *Molly Fisk*

The initial idea for *Open to All* was hatched on a return trip with Molly Fisk from a Poets & Writers regional meeting in Sacramento in early 2003. Molly was filling in the numerous gaps in my knowledge of Nevada County writers, past and present, and I mentioned a couple of library fund-raising book-publishing projects I'd worked on. Molly is one of Nevada County's favorite literary daughters. I mentioned to Steve Sanfield, another of the county's literary luminaries and the long-time director of The Sierra Storytelling Festival, that Molly and I had bounced around the idea of a literary anthology—containing submissions of Nevada County residents from all walks of life, augmented by the works of others dear to Nevada County and its environs. The idea started to snowball after we were able to enlist the talents and commitment of Dave Comstock, author, historian, and publisher of Comstock

Bonanza Press. The Nevada County Library Foundation agreed to steward the proceeds which would be used to buy books for all Nevada County Libraries. Dixie Redfearn and Soumitro Sen of *The Union*, along with Dave Bloch, the MyNevadaCounty.com webmaster, graciously offered their talents and energies to help us get the word out. Then all we needed was the enthusiasm of the community.

—*Steve Fjeldsted*

In many varied conversations among ourselves we realized we all shared a love of words. And their final repository, the book. And further the final repository of the book, the library—a place where we have spent and continue to spend a good deal of our time. From this sharing grew the idea of hearing what others remembered and cherished about libraries and their keepers, the librarians, past and present.

— *Steve Sanfield*

Acknowledgments

Our heartfelt thanks to all the staff and volunteers of the Nevada County Libraries; the Friends of the Library; the Nevada County Library Foundation; Debbie Cook, Mary Ann Trygg, and Claire Stafford in the Madelyn Helling Library; Steve Baker, Mike Thornton, and Eric Tomb of KVMR; Dixie Redfearn, Soumitro Sen, Pat Butler, and Jeff Ackerman of *The Union*; KNCO; YubaNet; Dave Comstock of Comstock Bonanza Press; Dave Bloch, Sarah Sparks, and Joy Fjeldsted.

Contents

Introductions: Fisk, Fjeldsted, Sanfield ... vi
Acknowledgments ... viii

Part I. A Well-Read Life

Madelyn Helling: After the Dawn ... 2
Sally Krause: Literary Manna by Mail ... 3
Gene Roghair: Wealth ... 4
David Mas Masumoto: Foreign Places ... 6
Miyoko Zwarich: A Heavenly Find ... 8
Gerald Haslam: What Horton Hatched ... 10
Jacquie Bellon: First Year Reading in America ... 12
Lydia Unruh: When You Go to the Library ... 13
Laura Pendell: St. Agnes Branch, New York City Public Library, 1956 ... 15
Nikko Wu: From Golden Fields to the Goldfields ... 16
Linda Menge: A Library Peace ... 18
Gail Entrekin: A Well-Read Life ... 19
Chuck Jaffee: Four Haiku ... 21
Meg Palley: Between the Covers ... 22
Nate Beason: Generations of Readers ... 23
Erica Light: World of Connections ... 24
Sands Hall: The Stacks ... 26
Gary Snyder: "The Books Are in the Library"— An Appreciation ... 28
Elizabeth Wilma McDaniel: Library Patrons ... 30
Lucille Lovestedt: The Realm of Unlimited Possibilities ... 31
Christine Irving: Only the Beginning ... 33
Nancy Williams: My Constant Companions ... 35
Ray Hadley: The Library Is Closed ... 36
Rosa Nieto: The Princesses of the Roseville Library ... 37
John Church: My Library Home ... 39
Alan Archer: Imagine That You Can't Read ... 41
Jeanie Harris: A Ticket to Anywhere ... 43
Mark Wilson: San Miguel de Allende, 2000 ... 45

Pamela Biery: Fair Haven Found　　　　　　　　　　46
Louis B. Jones: The Library　　　　　　　　　　　48
Soumitro Sen: The Phantom of the Library　　　　51
Rosanne Stratigakes: Before and After　　　　　　53
Jeff Ackerman: The Need to Know More　　　　　54
Gage McKinney: With the In-Crowd of Readers　　56
Charles Entrekin: The Award　　　　　　　　　　58
Janet Ann Collins: At Home in the Library　　　　60
Jean McKeen: Four Poems　　　　　　　　　　　62

Part II. Keepers of the Culture

Iven Lourie: Library Thoughts　　　　　　　　　　64
Steve Sanfield: Thank You Miss Groub　　　　　　66
Marilyn Harris Kriegel: Library　　　　　　　　　70
Steve Fjeldsted: The Key That Keeps On Turning　71
Dennis Carr: A Utopian Democracy　　　　　　　73
Chris Casey: Miss Whatever　　　　　　　　　　75
Glennis M. Dole: The Best of Times　　　　　　　78
Dale Jacobson: Keepers of the Culture　　　　　　80
Mary Ann Trygg: How to Catch a Match　　　　　82
Robert Lobell: Right There in the Stacks　　　　　84
Malcolm Margolin: Two Kisses　　　　　　　　　85
Molly Fisk: Not Studying　　　　　　　　　　　　87
Barbara Jones: Heartfelt Expression　　　　　　　89
Pam Jung: How Do I Love the Library? Let Me Count
　the Ways　　　　　　　　　　　　　　　　　　90
Suzanne Koliche: A Brief Reverie　　　　　　　　91
Arianne Wing: A Place to Dream the Impossible　 92
Anne Lamott: Good Friday World　　　　　　　　94
Utah Phillips: Ethiopia　　　　　　　　　　　　　95
Lucinda Sahm deLorimier: Dogs　　　　　　　　　97
Kate Dwyer: Good Dogs, Good Books　　　　　　99
Roo Cantada: the only quiet moment is before I open
　the library　　　　　　　　　　　　　　　　　101
Pat Black: Closing In　　　　　　　　　　　　　103
Judy Mariuz: The Long and Winding Road to Becoming a
　Librarian　　　　　　　　　　　　　　　　　　104
Catherine Allen: Misreading　　　　　　　　　　106

Part III. Anything Can Happen

M. M. Johnson: My Second World	108
Cathy Wilcox-Barnes: Summers at the Library	110
Maria Brower: Miss Pickerel Goes to Mars	112
Tom Taylor: Blessings	114
Chris Olander: Finding Me in the Library	116
Julian Eisen: My Favorite Place in Nevada County	118
Dick Phillips: A Case of Mistaken Identity	119
Edwin L. Tyson: My First Library Encounter	120
Priscilla van der Pas: The Library of Peter van der Pas	122
A. J. Leis: On Keeping Books	125
Dee Murphy: Longing to Be Della Street	126
Harold Berliner: Why I Like the Library	128
Peter Collier: For Laverne, Excerpt from Remarks at Her Memorial Service	130
Mary Volmer: Nana's Library	133
Sue Cauhape: Shelving	135
Todd Cirillo: One Afternoon in the Grass Valley Library	136

Part IV. The Day I Wandered In

Kelly Kolar Valin: The Library Book Sale	138
Britta Tigan: The Day I Wandered In	140
Myrna Courtney: Those Rows and Rows of Books	141
Emma V. Wall: Home Again	143
Elizabeth Unruh: Treasure Hunting	145
Ruby Totten: Too Much Reading	147
Donna Hanelin: Sting	148
Dale Pendell: What We Remember	150
C. B. Follett: The Library at Ephesus, at Alexandria	152
Richard Stockton: I Was a Feral Child Raised by Republicans	153
Gina Gippner: Close to Heaven	155
Cheryl Klein: Lost and Gone Forever	156
Judie Rae: Luddite in the Library	158
David H. Fenimore: The Library Is Dead	160
Ray Bradbury: Afterword	162
Nevada County Library Foundation	164
Friends of the Library	164
Friends of the Truckee Library	164

Illustrations

Elaine May Channel	v
Mary Street: Flying Books	14
Joan Brown: Doris Foley Library	22
John Church: Reading in the Pool	40
Rachel Unruh: Checking Out Books	77
Joan Brown: Josiah Royce Library	96
Linda Neely: Castle	102
Loana Beeson: Doris Foley Library	109
Suzanne Olive: Dappled Light on Linden Trees	113
George Mathis: Searls Law Office	121
Peter van der Pas	123
Loana Beeson: Josiah Royce Library	127
Linda Pearson: Anything Can Happen	129
Laverne Vaughan	132
Tyler Micoleau: The Linden Tree	139
Library Quilt	146
Ray Bradbury	163

Part I. A Well-Read Life

After the Dawn
MADELYN HELLING

Pure and simple, books mean everything to me. They always have, and I expect they always will. My school did not have a library, so I discovered the Bismarck Public Library, much to my happiness. It was a place of discovery and I don't recall anyone on the staff giving me any ideas on what to read or asking me about what I picked out. I just browsed the stacks reading subjects and fiction from A to Z, finding a wonderful variety of authors, such as my all-time favorite *Kristin Lavransdatter* by Nobel Prize winner Sigrid Undset.

In high school my mother said I should be a librarian since I had my nose in a book all the time. It didn't register seriously with me at the time, but it must have made a strong subliminal impression, ready to surface at the right time. After college and working for airlines for some thirteen years I remembered reading that one should do as a vocation what one likes as an avocation. The light dawned! My love of reading and belief in the importance of everyone reading ignited my missionary zeal to reach people. Then off to UC-Berkeley Graduate Library School I went. My whole life changed for the better.

Each day working in a library one is opened up to the joy of new ideas, helping and understanding people, increasing one's knowledge, an appreciation for the freedom to read in a democracy, and a willingness to fight for these. Who could not love being a librarian?

How could I ever thank the Bismarck Public Library enough and a patient mother who let me read so much, didn't question anything I was reading, and paid my library overdue fines without complaint?

Madelyn Helling is a retired Nevada County Librarian

Literary Manna By Mail

SALLY KRAUSE

MY first experience with a public library was a long distance one. I grew up in a very small North Dakota town by the Canadian border. The nearest public library was 50 miles away, but in those days, in the '30s and '40s, our family didn't make trips that far away except for visits to relatives or for medical appointments. Our school had a limited library, which my sisters and I quickly exhausted. A few of the older residents in the town had book collections and allowed us to borrow from them.

Then my mother remembered that the State Library in Bismarck offered a fine service, one she had used as a child on the farm in eastern North Dakota. She sent the librarian our ages and a list of what we liked to read. In about a week, a big box of books came by mail, several for each of us. When we finished reading them, we'd send them back—we had to pay the return postage—and soon another box would be at the post office. The librarian kept track of what we read, and we never got a repeat. Years later one of my sisters used the same service for her children when they lived in another small town without a library. Three generations of our family had used that library-by-mail program.

It was a godsend for children like us, whose parents nurtured our love of reading.

Sally Krause lives in Penn Valley

Wealth

GENE ROGHAIR

MY grade school was in Okaton, population forty-seven. The view from Okaton was limited by the curvature of the earth and unobstructed by any visible trees; six miles to the south was a dark line I knew to be cottonwoods along the White River. Like every Milwaukee Road town from the Missouri to the Black Hills, Okaton sprang up in 1906-07. Its early optimism manifested itself in a stucco structure with four classrooms, a gymnasium, and combined woodshop and chemistry lab. Along with the rest of the town and surrounding farms, this school lacked plumbing of any kind. Toilets opened directly into an inexhaustible pit under one corner of the building. Lime was ready at hand. By 1952, when I enrolled, the high school was history: one teacher and eight grades occupied a single room, but books still lined the walls of the former principal's office.

During first grade, on the day before Christmas vacation, I found readers for several grades stored in the cloakroom, took them home and read them. Back at school, the teacher was usually preoccupied with other students; there was little to interfere with my education. An hour or two in the morning sufficed for schoolwork, and I was free to begin my reading for the day. Within a couple of years I had read all the books in the classroom: Laura Ingalls Wilder, colonial and American biographies, and a series concerning young athletes who came through in the clutch. *Blue Ridge Billy* was a favorite, *Conquest of Everest* an inspiration. That's when I discovered the wonders of *Webster's New International* at the back of the room and *Britannica* and *World Book* in the hall.

By about fourth grade, I received a key and unrestricted access to the principal's office. The walls were lined with the likes of Twain, Poe, Cooper, Stevenson, Bunyan, and Kipling. There were *Heidi, Pinocchio, Peter Pan, Sherlock Holmes, Robin Hood, Pee Wee Harris*, and more. Many were challenging, but *The Scarlet Letter* made no sense and I never finished it. My reading strategy was simple. Most days I selected a book by 9:30 AM and read all day except for noon and recess. When I got home, I stretched out on my bed and read until I had to feed the hogs and milk the cow. When the supper dishes were done, I read until Dad called up the stairs for me to turn off the light.

Fortunately, the school library was only a beginning. At home my dad read the Bible, a chapter a day, from Genesis through Revelations at the supper table. I absorbed the whole thing, including Numbers and The Song of Solomon, twice before I was twelve. Selective Bible reading has seemed misleading to me ever since. All the Bible reading was complemented by my mother's *Handbook of Children's Literature,* which introduced the gods of the Greeks, Romans, and Norse. It also provided folktales and fairytales from all over the world. Our home library included *McCall's, Farm Journal,* and *Popular Science,* which I read more or less cover-to-cover. Grandma passed on *Post, Look, National Geographic,* and memorable books like *Life of an American Workman* by Walter P. Chrysler. As a *Grit* newspaper salesman, I read that as well. While waiting to move the truck for my dad and uncles at wheat harvest time, I read *Reader's Digest* in the cab of the International. Book Club selections at home included *Mutiny on the Bounty* and *Kon Tiki,* inspiring corncob rafts on our stock pond.

Murdo, county seat with a population of 500, had a hole in the wall of the courthouse where I got Tarzan and Zane Grey books. It also had mesmerizing books about exploring the Amazon. In Pierre, the State capital with a population of 5000, I visited the State Library, but I never got to stay very long. I always got books about the history of boats and ships.

These many libraries worked well for me, but the reading needs of my friend, Alvis (later Elvis), were not addressed. Like the students named Ghost and Woman Dress, Elvis and the other Crazy Bears spoke no English at home and had no books. We rode our horses and played basketball together, but on many levels our lives did not intersect. The teachers and educational system were generally not a positive experience for these Sioux classmates. The libraries were in someone else's language.

Gene Roghair of Grass Valley is a Telugu scholar and salesman

Foreign Places

DAVID MAS MASUMOTO

MY Baachan/Grandmother was a farm worker, an immigrant from Japan in the early 1900s who never stepped into a library. She never knew books. She could not read. But she kept a bundle of letters, kept tucked safely away in the back of her dresser drawer. Wrapped in a faded white muslin cloth, a tan string with frayed ends securely bound the collection together. Some were written in English, most in Japanese. I was shocked to discover she could not read them.

I recall family friends coming to visit and together they'd read the letters. Typically, it was an Issei (first generation Japanese American) man who read the letters. His eyes moved up and down and his head seemed to nod as he read, completing one line and moving back up to the next. Together they heard information from a distant homeland, news from a native village, words from far away families.

Baachan kept these letters alongside her alien registration card and the purple heart from the US Army after her oldest son died fighting in France during World War II. Without translation, though, all the writing, either in English or Japanese, must have appeared as dark scratches on pieces of paper.

I discovered she was illiterate when I asked her to write our family name in Japanese. I had set out a blank sheet of white paper and a pencil in front of her. I gently pushed a pencil into her old, calloused hand and gestured her to write. My Japanese language skills were so limited, I couldn't ask more than say, "Namae Kudasai/Name please, Baachan."

She blinked back, her old eyes dull. She awkwardly squeezed the slender wood and it slipped from her bony fingers. I picked it up again and placed it in her hand. Her old hand shook as she gamely tried to write. Her fingers turned white as she gripped the pencil tightly. The lead point pierced the paper and tore through, leaving behind a few rough scratches and a hole. She put the pencil down and looked away.

Why would she keep something she could never read? I believe she felt they were sacred: each letter held stories. Her stack of letters were the only window into another world she had left behind. Perhaps she valued them even more because she could not read.

Immigrating to a new land, scarred by the World War II relocation of Japanese Americans, she would always feel alien. I imagine her walking into a library, another foreign place where she didn't belong. Each book contained a new universe of different places and people, but she could not unlock them: she lacked the passport of literacy.

Perhaps reading could have helped her connect with her adopted land. I believe if she knew how to read she would have enjoyed libraries. I recall as a child, watching her looking at old magazines, studying the pictures. Places could have come alive if she could read the caption. Books could have helped transport her into stories of other lives and communities. Libraries and their stacks of books may have become a sacred place for my Baachan.

My grandmother knew the value of words, that's why she kept those letters. She treasured them not for herself but for another generation, her children and grandchildren who could read and would be able to step into her world, even if just for a moment through letters of an immigrant.

Even though libraries were a lost world for her, I believe she understood the potential joy of books as she watched her grandchildren devour books. She was grateful that another generation would be given the key to unlock all those stories and journey to new places she would never know. Words, books, and libraries could have completed her.

David Mas Masumoto is a multi award-winning author who lives and works in Del Rey, California; his Epitaph for a Peach *was the centerpiece of the 2006 "Nevada County Reads" project; parts of this appeared in* The Fresno Bee, *April 2006*

A Heavenly Find

MIYOKO ZWARICH

IT was about twenty years ago when I came to Nevada County from Japan. And what did I find in this heavenly county? The endless rolling hills wrapped around my soul with warm green arms, and the powerful gong-like sound of Yuba River washed off my busy mind, I immersed myself into the deep meditation of a country life. I thought: *This is Heaven! If we can't find Heaven here, we will never find it anywhere.*

After a long hike, enjoying the golden orange California poppies on both sides of the hill, my husband and I usually read books by the riverside. I felt hiking and reading would keep our minds and bodies in top condition!

Reflecting upon my life in Japan, I seldom had time to read books in a quiet place—my reading time was only in the crowded train or bus. Here, listening to nature's song, my mind became calm enough to read.

At first I read only Japanese books which my mom and friends had sent from Japan, but my English never progressed that way. I was frustrated when a salesman asked me over the phone, "Can you speak in English?"

"Can't you understand my English?" Furiously, I hung up.

I realized how bad my English was. I said to myself: *Nobody can understand what I say; I'm a handicapped person here! I must master English. From now on I will read only English books rather than Japanese ones.*

It was my turning point. From then on I started reading only English books which my mentor and friend, Nancy, chose for me from condensed classical literature. I was carried away by the eminent authors' excellent stories such as *Crime and Punishment, A Tale of Two Cities, Great Expectations, The Scarlet Letter, Anna Karenina, Jane Eyre, Wuthering Heights,* etc.

Then my husband introduced me to the Grass Valley Library in the old gold mining town. As I entered the dignified classic building with its red brick façade, highlighted with white pilasters, a peculiar thought came into my mind: *How many gold miners stepped into the library? Maybe the library books filled the lonely gold miner's hearts with joy ... but if they couldn't read, what would their lives be like—spending their lives just digging, drinking, and gambling?*

The library was replete with many different kinds of books, as well as videotapes, audio books, and CDs. I brought back a bagful of the audio books and the videotapes for my listening and visual training every week. While working in the kitchen or garden and even hiking, I listened to the audio books, and my speaking and understanding of English improved year-by-year.

All the librarians welcomed me with big smiles whenever I visited, and they talked to me in a friendly way, so I felt at home there. One librarian asked me, "Do you have a Japanese-English Dictionary?"

"No, I only have an English-Japanese one," I replied.

"So, this is for you," she smiled, handing me a big dictionary.

"Are you sure?" My mouth dropped open with surprise when I saw it.

"Of course, nobody uses it here except you."

"I desperately wanted it, but I couldn't find it. Thank you very much."

I was so glad to have the Japanese-English Dictionary since I was always puzzled by not knowing how to express my feelings in English properly.

It also became a great tool for writing stories as Nancy corrected my grammatical errors. Later I enrolled in autobiography and poetry classes at Sierra College. Those teachers were very skillful. And then I joined the Sierra Writing Club. Most of the members in the club had already published their stories or articles, and they were kind enough to give me some hints about writing techniques. Little by little I'm learning how to write a story. And now I've almost finished my long story called *War and Peace in a Japanese Family*.

Reading and writing fed my hungry soul and helped fulfill my dream of mastering English. But without the kind librarians and my gentle friends, I would have been lost in the middle of a wilderness, holding Japanese books under my arm, or floating on the Yuba River bumping my head on the rocks not knowing where I was going.

I still have a long way to go, but at least I can see the way to get there. In this heavenly county, I found the beautiful people that showed me the way.

Miyoko Zwarich lives in Penn Valley

What Horton Hatched

GERALD W. HASLAM

MY earliest memory is of sitting on my mother's lap listening to *Horton Hatches the Egg:*

> "I meant what I said
> And I said what I meant
> an elephant's faithful
> one hundred percent...."

As the only child of a working class family during the Great Depression, I was read to constantly, and sung to constantly, and talked to constantly. Language and imagination were my companions.

Books in particular came to be magical instruments to me. My folks didn't own many volumes, but my mother visited the Oildale branch of the Kern County Library weekly, frequently taking me with her. There I gazed at illustrated editions while she made her choices—both children's and adult's books each visit. As nearly as I can recall, she always allowed me one choice of my own.

Those books were revered in our house, often read aloud, frequently discussed by the adults, and I was taught to read before beginning classes at Standard School. As soon as I acquired my own library card—a rite of passage in my family rivaled only when I received my driver's license ten years later—I became a regular at our neighborhood library.

There I, like my pals, was encouraged and directed by generous ladies who seemed to believe that all we barefooted, we burnished, we generally disheveled kids were worthy of their hope. What we couldn't recognize (but those librarians certainly did) as we dug through dinosaur books and pirate yarns, was that we had begun the process of sharing the accumulated wisdom of our culture ... indeed, of our species. That idea was far too remote and elevated to have crossed our minds at the time.

But that is exactly what we—we Okies, we Bloods, we Chili-Chokers ... whatever we were called then—were doing: building the foundation that has allowed us to participate in our shared culture. And in doing so, we have changed and shaped it. In our cultural hearts, we are all part African, all part Asian, all part European, all part of everything that filled those books that stirred our minds.

For me it started with a faithful elephant sitting on a lazy bird's egg and with my mother's voice. Sadly, Mom is no longer with us, but that egg continues hatching, a library's enduring legacy: mother to son, son to granddaughter, granddaughter to ... the world, faithful, one hundred percent.

What Horton hatched for me was my life.

Gerald W. Haslam of Penngrove, California, has written more than two dozen fiction and nonfiction books; he has been called "The Prince of California"

First Year Reading in America

JACQUIE BELLON

IT'S Fall 1953, in Los Angeles, I'm twelve years old and have been in America for 9 months. I'm in the 7th grade at Bancroft Junior High. My English is pretty good after having spent a few months in a small private school in the spring, then summer camp, followed by a short stint in a Catholic school. But I still prefer to read in French, so every week or two my mother takes me to the Beverly Hills Library where I can find French language books.

It's a Saturday morning and my mother and I are walking along Santa Monica Boulevard toward the stucco Spanish-style library, resplendent in white, set on a wide lawn and surrounded by flowering geraniums. Behind us is a clutch of girls my age talking and laughing out loud. They're laughing at me and mocking me, I know it. Drenched in shame, a blade of ice coursing through my body, I try to explain to my mother that they are laughing because I am dressed funny; that this happens at school every day she sends me off wearing the above-the-knee, frilly little-girl dresses she has made for me. All the girls are dressed in calf-length straight skirts and matching sweater sets. I dread going to school where I'm the odd duck and a very easy target in my all too short outfits. I just want to be like everyone else and blend in and be popular. I want to be an American, not a little French girl.

Because we are walking together and the girls behind us are laughing, my mother experiences herself the gauntlet I run every day. Before we reach the library she turns to them and says something sharp which only serves to humiliate me more. I'm grateful when we finally reach the quiet, welcoming spaciousness of the library where no one looks up or talks or laughs. Jules Verne, Victor Hugo, and Alexandre Dumas are shelved together in a cozy section. I find my old friends and take them home with me to delight in their delicious company.

Jacquie Bellon is an artist and teacher living on the San Juan Ridge

When You Go to the Library

LYDIA UNRUH

When you go to the library to get a good book,
Go to the shelves and take a good look.
Look at the books, pick one you will like.
It could be about cats, dogs, or taking a hike.
When you find a good book but can't check it out,
Find the librarian, she'll help you out.
You need to have a library card.
You can go get one, it's not very hard.
Then you go home, turn on a bright light,
Make yourself tea, and read through the night.

Lydia Unruh, Grass Valley, age 10

Flying Books. *Pencil Drawing by Mary Street*

St. Agnes Branch, NYC Public Library, 1956

LAURA PENDELL

Every two weeks I return to those soft pages—
limp, aged to ochre, velvet in my hands.
I fill my arms with books, steady them
with my chin, all seven of them, the limit
a girl of ten can check out with her
cherished blue library card. Too young to walk
the nine blocks of busy city streets alone,
my mother makes time to take me
to the old grey stone building
with its steep steps and heavy wooden door.

Inside, my treasures: shelves of titles,
well-used, bruised, with a funny smell.
I scan each row for something
the way another child might
walk the beach looking for new shells.

Then home and quickly to my hideaway:
the deep closet in the back bedroom.
I slide behind hanging coats and dresses,
nestle into the cardboard box filled with
heavy purple drapes. A bare light bulb
on a chain above my head. Just enough
room for a small girl and a book. A safe place
for reading: both refuge and entrance
into lands far away from here.

Laura Pendell lives in Penn Valley

From Golden Fields to the Goldfields

NIKKO WU

IF I could pick any type of dwelling, I'd live inside a library because I'd be surrounded by so much wisdom. Whenever I'd want I could hand pick from the vast array of books. Then I could be transported to so many places of my choosing and even other states of mind. Reading liberates me from the bounds of space and time and lures me into different dimensions. When I'm involved with a book, I'm drinking from the author's thoughts and ideas. They enter my bloodstream and permeate my skin. Wonderful written words can move my heart and compel my soul to dance with delight. My senses can even become sharpened, as when I breathe in the heavenly scent of books.

Maybe that's why I've become an avid book collector. My favorite subjects are philosophy, spiritual healing, self-improvement, and Chinese and English language poetry. But I could never amass the number of selections of an entire library. Even though I'm the caretaker of my personal collection, such wasn't always the case. Life was so simple when I was growing up in a quiet village on the tropical isle of Taiwan. Golden rice paddies were a lot more plentiful than elegant writings. My hometown's name, San-Sha, means three gorges because it's located at the crossing of tributaries of the Yang-Ze River.

From the time I was seven years old, I'd get up before sunrise to cook for the whole family. Meals were prepared in an oversized wok that was so big I'd have to be careful not to fall in. We hauled our laundry to the river and pounded it on rocks, before hanging it to dry on bamboo sticks. I'd routinely lead our stubborn, big-eyed buffalo into the field, before it was time to leave for school. My introduction to the outside world came from the box of books my teacher pulled out after class as a reward. This was my first encounter with anything even slightly resembling a library. I can remember once feeling my heartbeat while my fingers touched the vividly colored pages.

Our teacher let each of us choose a book to take home. Once there, evening chores included returning the buffalo to his straw bale shed and feeding the noisy pigs, chickens, and ducks before carrying water in bamboo buckets from our pond to irrigate the vegetable garden. Usually by then it was time to cook dinner. Afterwards I needed to complete my homework before I could open my storybook. Then I could enter a totally different reality. By the time I closed the cover I was ready to drift off to sleep until I'd be awakened by a rooster's crow piercing the monotonic rhythms of the crickets and bullfrogs.

The first real library I ever visited—a journey requiring a two-hour walk—was during middle school. At closing time I'd linger until the librarian kicked me out. My dream then was to someday become a librarian so I could stay and read all the books.

My family had a vegetable garden, a fruit orchard, and bamboo forest land, mainly for food and building. Our tiny two-bedroom mud house was cramped with three generations. I started saving pennies to purchase my own books and didn't want to buy frilly clothes or shoes like most girls. When the walls became crowded with the books I purchased, my Grandma cautioned me that women should only learn enough to be able to read, but they should never think for themselves.

Nowadays my home is in the Nevada County foothills. But instead of being an early bird like my parents I'm much more of a night owl. I look forward to staying up late, deep into the wee hours, enchanted by a book. If my industrious parents could see me now they might consider me somewhat of a lazy bookworm. When I wake up in the morning to the sound of a book hitting the floor, I love to step outside. Drawing in a full breath, I'll gaze at the silhouette of the mountains and the sunshine starting to glisten on the morning dew.

Now, as my hands touch the keyboard, I wonder what's happened to me. What was the catalyst of my transformation from a farmer's daughter to a bookworm? My grandma warned me what could happen if I got lost in books. I think she was right! But no matter what, I know I'm getting the best from my time, continually learning more while my spirit soars.

Nikko Wu lives in Cedar Ridge

A Library Peace

LINDA MENGE

I READ my first book there on the Bookmobile steps, Dr. Seuss of course: *One Fish Two Fish*. I was so proud!! I decided then and there that I wanted to read every book ever written. I could only get four books at a time though—so it was going to take a while. I got my own library card in the third grade. In retrospect it was more coveted than my driver's license at 16!

I didn't know what a real library was until way later. The Bookmobile was our lifeline to the outside. Every two weeks, on Tuesday at 2:30, the Bookmobile would wind its way through the towering redwoods to our little community. We would anxiously wait for it. If it was only a few minutes late it seemed like forever. The trip for him took only 45 minutes—but his short trip enabled us to experience the world.

A family of nine, we very rarely left home. Our big outing was walking down the hill to meet the Bookmobile, a library outreach to secluded rural areas. I loved the smell of the Bookmobile, the crackle of the plastic-covered books, the neat little pockets on the inside cover that held the checkout card, and the way the librarian stamped each book with the date. (Don't be late!!) Such a great system!

The interior wheel wells served as "seats" for two or three little bodies—voraciously picking though pages and avidly consuming illustrations and text as if it were thick creamy cheesecake after the Lenten season. Skylights spotlighted favorite books. We checked out Dr. Seuss week after week, because we could *really* read them.

The librarian was a cool, suave "Frankie" type: starched white dress shirt, rolled-up sleeves, open and unbuttoned (showing almost too much chest hair), slacks, and faintly smelling of cigarettes. Big smile; piano teeth. I always thought he had a crush on Mom, but maybe the perceived love was simply a shared love of books?

Sitting on the steps of the Bookmobile, hugging/holding my books as if I let up they would run away and escape me like a feral cat, we waited impatiently for Mom to finish talking and laughing with "Frankie." Then we would march back up the hill with our cargo, as if we had gotten away with something, and a sense of peace would come over us: a Library Peace.

Linda Menge lives in Grass Valley

A Well-Read Life

GAIL RUDD ENTREKIN

MY mother sat, as she so often did, on the dark green front porch swing, the rose-covered trellis that blocked the view of the neighbors deeply shading her, and as she rocked, she read from her current library book. A glass of iced tea sat on the round metal table beside her. That's the vision I hold.

She went through a book or more a week, novels mostly, and she never discussed those books with me, or anyone, as far as I know. It was her private world, her escape from the craziness of our lives, her adventures that compensated in some measure for having settled down to a low-key, low-income life in Lakewood, Ohio.

We owned only one small set of books on the built-in shelves beside the fireplace, almost all of them my dad's from earlier years when he was still a reader. I had already read them all so, like my mother, I made the short trip to the library every week, especially during the summer, when I sometimes read as many as three books a week. While the main library had a larger selection, it was farther away, so I often walked to the closer Madison branch, which happened to be located next door to the public pool. That way I could switch books, then lie out by the pool and read all afternoon. I had a summer pass for the pool, a small silver disk that my mom sewed to my suit at the beginning of each summer, the one expenditure she allowed us as it offered her freedom from us all those long summer afternoons.

Flash ahead forty years. I am visiting my mom in her assisted-living apartment on Leisure Lane. On her coffee table sits the usual stack of three glossy-covered novels. As always, we don't talk about them, but she sits long into the night by her jade lamp in her green velvet chair, reading, escaping from the confines of her one and only life. In the morning the Bookmobile is due, so she wants to finish this book and turn it in.

At 10 a.m. she is ready. We get her books and walk, slowly, slowly, admiring the roses on the neighbor's patio, the climatis covering the doorway outside the dining room. There sits the little bus in the parking lot, and the elderly, mostly infirm, are moving slowly toward it from all directions of the complex. We are the first ones this morning, and the librarian, who knows my mother, steps down and helps her up the step. She has a book she's been saving for her. It has her name on it: Virginia.

They are on a first-name basis. I am introduced and we chat briefly while my mother selects two more books. She does so quickly, as a half dozen others are waiting and there's only enough room in the bus for one or two people at a time.

It has been years since Mom could drive. She is 92 years old. The facility's bus takes her to the grocery store and the bank. But what would she do without the Bookmobile? As we slowly inch our way back across the parking lot, Mom grins at me, pats her canvas bag of books and says jauntily, "Some fun in here now, kiddo." Yeah, Mom. Some fun.

Gail Rudd Entrekin of Nevada City is a founding member of Literature Alive! Her newest book is Change Will Do You Good

Four Haiku

CHUCK JAFFEE

holding Mommy's hand
first look at the library
doorway to doorways

- - - -

a homeless old man
sits on a library couch
reads a newspaper

- - - -

summer; John Steinbeck
and that librarian knew
I'd be back for more

- - - -

Google is faster
it just doesn't smell the same
as thousands of books

Chuck Jaffee is a poet, movie reviewer, technical writer, and President of the Sierra Writers Group

Between the Covers

MEG PALLEY

I WAS declared legally able to drive my car again when Dr. Hagele said my vision showed improvement. My first trip yesterday was to the library, where I found doors open at ten (money spent for war shortens library hours available), so after stopping for the gas station and getting money at the bank, I return and take out the book I had reserved. Granny D. walks across the country at 90, protesting end of democracy as money buys the elections. (I shall start walking more today at 88.)

As I read, I learn the possibility that one dedicated person can change attitudes of many. I, too, want rights of people to come before rights of wealth.

We need adequately staffed libraries that invite all to come learn.

Books were the reward we gave our kids if the dental trip showed no cavities.

Libraries are places I am drawn to when visiting a new city or town. There I meet people who read and think: some in person, others between the covers of a book.

Meg Palley of Nevada City is a life-long activist, still active at 89

Doris Foley Library. *Drawing by Joan Brown.*

Generations of Readers

NATE BEASON

Having had the benefit of undergraduate and graduate education at two superb universities, one public, one private, I often reflect on the path my life took toward higher education and where it all started. I began using the local library in my hometown of 4,000 souls when I was about eight years of age. Although a community of blue-collar workers of relatively modest means, my parents' and grandparents' generations were keen on ensuring as many opportunities as possible for their children to gain access to as many forms of education as possible. You might say that their corporate goal was to provide every means for their children to avoid doing what they had to do to make a living. In many of our cases, our parents succeeded well beyond their wildest expectations.

The public library's summer reading program was my first formal educational venue. I can remember walking with my friends approximately one mile on those bright San Joaquin Valley days to the library, where we read and checked out books. We were given stars of various colors as we gained in number of books read—green, red, blue, silver, and, at last, gold. Year after year, as we grew older and started using the school libraries as well as the public one, reading for pleasure and learning evolved into an internalized process. Education became a natural endeavor in which no level of knowledge was thought to be unachievable. We were also involved in sports, music, the arts, cars, and part-time jobs, but rarely were we far from a book or books where a read was in progress.

It is my profound conviction that without libraries in my life, my basic and advanced education would have taken a different turn, or at least a longer path. This is the gift of a robust library system with access for all. The legacy of the gift, in my particular case, is the imbedded value my children, and in turn my grandchildren, place on reading. It is a family tradition.

In this time of rapid technological devices and instant information, there is no proper substitute for sitting quietly with a good book and letting your imagination or your mind's eye create, among other things, its own picture of the author's message.

Nate Beason of Nevada City is a Nevada County Supervisor

World of Connections

ERICA LIGHT

LIBRARIES are about making connections: connecting folks with information, citizens with their neighbors and communities, authors with readers and scholars with their global network. My world has always included at least one library. In our family books were collected, respected, read and loved. In grade school, roller skates, bike or saddle shoes took me to our neighborhood branch library a few short blocks from home. Hushed, dimly lit, and presided over by an intimidating personage known as "the librarian," it drew me into its cool and reverent atmosphere. A pale peach-colored, hand-typed library card was my prized passport to Nancy Drew, Laura Ingalls Wilder, and the exotic destinations of the *National Geographic*.

In college, later on, the campus libraries provided a calm retreat from outside distractions. I spent leisurely hours flipping through the card catalogue and perusing the dusty volumes, tracking down a key quote or verifying a page number or footnote. The library connected students to one another and provided a portal to "what had come before"—in our case, the history of art. As a grad student I worked part-time in the slide and photograph collection, part of our departmental library. It was there one afternoon, while sorting, cleaning and filing slides, that I made a very special connection; I met my future husband.

Later still, research drew me to libraries far from home. Access to the hallowed halls of art historical reference libraries in New York, Florence, and Rome required formal letters of introduction. Long-sought bibliographic treasures appeared on polished tabletops in silent, high-ceilinged, pencils-only reading rooms. Every hour was precious and excitement accompanied each visit. Here connections were made with other scholars; generations of them had occupied the heavy, well-worn wooden chairs. You might even have found yourself sitting across from the author of the article you were reading!

Primary research ultimately took me to the Archivio di Stato in Siena, where hundreds of years of civic records are preserved in a Quattrocento palace, some of which may not have seen the light of day since their ink dried. Every moment of my nine-month search through folders of 15th-century handwritten documents had all the excitement of a treasure hunt. I connected with "my" Sienese painter and his world through the carefully recorded details of his life. Marriage agreements, commissions for painted work and tax records helped to flesh out his re-emerging persona. The stone-cold chill of the reading room contrasted deliciously with warm sun and pizza at lunch each day with fellow researchers in the Piazza del Campo. Five hundred years before, the folks who had recorded their connections in the documents we sought worked, walked, laughed, lived in this piazza under the same warm sun. Our search connected us with people who lived there before. Results of the work done in all these libraries produced articles in the following years; later these will help others to make their own connections with the past.

When I left academia and got reacquainted with our public libraries I was reminded of how essential they have become to our community connectedness. Library cards had become bar-coded plastic and library staff far more friendly and approachable. When our boys were small, another, cozier, neighborhood branch library welcomed their pursuit of hungry caterpillars, cats in hats and adventurous tank engines. Our schools kept small libraries and, after we came to Nevada County a decade ago, I volunteered at our middle school library. Connections made there later inspired me to seek an assistant position at Nevada County Library where I now help folks to find the information they need, to make their connections, from the other side of the desk.

Erica Light lives in North San Juan and is a Library Assistant for Nevada County Library

The Stacks

SANDS HALL

IN Squaw Valley, California, before the 1960 Olympics arrived to put the place on the map, the available library was my parents' extensive collection of books. Tahoe Lake Elementary, seven miles away, offered a sunlit room where books and the volumes of an encyclopedia slanted this way and that on painted shelves, but the books at home were plentiful and more fun: in fourth grade I wrote an illustrated paper on "The Wines of France," taken largely from the glossy book of that name that sat on our coffee table. I learned the shapes of glassware appropriate for wines white and red, for champagne and aperitif, although I would not taste what went in them for another decade or so.

Although of course I used the library (I like that "the library" describes a specific place as well as the generality of libraries) through grammar and high school and at various universities, it took me a surprisingly long time to appreciate what a library is. In the meantime, what impressed me was that someone in the past had found the muscle and money to build such edifices. I would pause in my forays across campus to stare at cornerstones, imagining the intention, the *vision* that went into a building large enough to house "The Stacks." That is my clearest memory of university libraries: trotting up and down stairs in search of the right room, the appropriate *wing*, then walking the equivalent of several city blocks, back and forth among floor-to-ceiling metal shelves, to match the letters and numbers on a book's spine to those scribbled on a piece of scratch paper.

This was all satisfying, but my affection, my passion, for the library took hold when I was researching my play, *Fair Use*. I had just discovered the connection between the life and letters of writer/illustrator Mary Hallock Foote and Wallace Stegner's *Angle of Repose*, and in order to compare the letters Stegner's fictional Susan Ward writes to a fictional friend to those Foote wrote to a real friend, I rose before dawn to drive to Stanford, where Foote's letters are housed in that library's Special Collection. It was necessary to order the desired documents by 9 a.m., then kick one's heels for several hours while they were fetched. Waiting (I looked forward to those letters; I was ferreting out a mystery!), I imagined a bespectacled, frock-coated minion trotting through underground shelves—I'd heard about Oxford's library, where the equivalent of golf carts are used to cover the literal miles of subterranean stacks. I thought about the fact that England has so much more history than America does, and imagined thick tomes of vellum, deep in the recesses of ancient shelves, that had not been looked at in centuries, but that were there, waiting, in a *library*, most likely catalogued in some way, if and when someone cared to open their dusty covers. And I was struck, dazzled, forever changed by the realization of the care, concern, passion, and organization that it takes to create and maintain a library:

> "A place in which literary and artistic materials ... are kept for reference or reading. A collection of such materials especially when systematically arranged for reference. An institution or foundation maintaining such a collection. From *booksellers shop*, from *book*."

Carrying the black document boxes to a table, carrying them as if they were jewels on a velvet pillow, I almost staggered with gratitude. History! Our past made present! All the documents: books, letters, sketches, graphs, maps, CDs, DVDs, future forms we can only guess at, the *records* of those who came before, available to those who come after. A library! Not just a place to borrow a book, but a temple—no wonder their ceilings are so often high—where the past can be rediscovered.

Lately I've had the pleasure of taking my nephew to the Madelyn Helling Library, where we crouch amongst the children's stacks and discuss books he might like to carry home. Dashiell has very particular tastes, shaking his head with certainty at one unopened offering, and practically pushing me over with his enthusiasm to turn the pages of another. Because of its welcoming atmosphere and convenience, he already has a good sense of what a library is and can offer. As he kneels beside me on the floor, too excited by the immediacy of This Book! to carry it to a table, I imagine the pleasures awaiting him and his children after him, not just in story books and fiction, but through research, and in history, when they discover cultures other than their own, and eras that precede their own: the world, in fact—all the journeys available in and through the library.

Sands Hall is an actor, director, playwright, and author whose publications include a novel, Catching Heaven

"The Books Are in the Library" — An Appreciation

GARY SNYDER

THE Library has a long history. It is an essential element in our Occidental humanistic and scientific tradition which has demonstrated such an extraordinary ability to maintain itself through time. The institution of the library is at the heart of that persistence.

Although Strabo said "Aristotle was the first man to have collected books," there were in truth hundreds of outstanding private libraries in Greece and throughout the Mediterranean of classical times. What survived of Aristotle's personal library became the basis of one of the first institutional libraries, which soon became a feature of classical civilization. There were of course far older libraries, and in the broader sense archives of literature and lore were kept world-wide, in virtually all cultures, whether they had writing or not.

The original context of teaching must have been narratives told by elders to young people gathered around the hearth fire. Our fascination with TV may just be nostalgia for that flickering light. In this huge old occidental culture, now our teaching elders are books. Books are almost our grandparents! In the library there are useful, demanding, and friendly elders available to us. I like to think of writers like Father Bartholomé de las Casas, whose sixteenth-century writings passionately defended the Indians of New Spain against his less scrupulous fellow Spaniards, or Baruch Spinoza, who defied the traditions of Amsterdam to become a true philosopher.

Making hoards and heaps, saving lore and information, is entirely natural: some archeologists have excavated the heaped-up woodrat nests out in the Mohave desert, packed full of little rodent treasures that are 12,000 years old. We humans are truly just beginners.

In our human case, the gathered "Information Nutrients" are stored in a place called the *bibliotek*, "place of the papyrus"—or the *library*, "place of bark," because the Latin word for tree-bark and book is the same, reflecting a memory of the earliest fiber used for writing material.

What lies behind it all is language. Language is a mind-body system that co-evolved with our needs and nerves. Like imagination and the body, language rises unbidden. It is of a complexity that eludes our rational intellectual capacities, yet the child learns the mother-tongue early and has virtually mastered it by six.

Such natural freshness and order-from-within, wonderful as it is, though, is only one part of the story. The amazing social and historical *deliberateness* that has maintained libraries made available to the public over the centuries is the other side of it, culminating in our American practice of libraries great and small throughout the nation. As a depression-era boy growing up on a dairy farm outside Seattle, our weekly trip to the northernmost branch of the Public Library was what trained and taught me to read and think, even more than school.

The fine Nevada County library system and its ever-growing outreach serves not just us locals, but contributes a bit to the sanity of world culture. I can't help but love libraries for their beautifully organized treasures of culture and knowledge, and their conviviality and welcoming spirit.

Gary Snyder is a Pulitzer Prize-winning poet living on the San Juan Ridge; based on an essay in A Place in Space, *1995*

Library Patrons

WILMA ELIZABETH McDANIEL

I well remember a Valley day
when the sparse San Joaquin rain
went wild
out of all self-control
and drenched us library patrons
before we reached the door
complaining to each other

Inside the grey man, as we call him
(with the faded blue eyes)
is reading *The New York Times*
his head covered by a
cocked hat
made from a newspaper

Wilma Elizabeth McDaniel, now in her 80s, lives in Tulare California; she's published more than two dozen books of poetry, and her works appear in numerous anthologies, including The Last Dust Storm

The Realm of Unlimited Possibilities

LUCILLE K. LOVESTEDT

SOMETIMES I arrive at the library a few minutes before it opens. Almost always there are other people waiting on the steps, and there is an immediate sense of fellowship amongst us, as if we might be prepared to give each other a secret handshake. We are an eager and expectant small group waiting for the **CLOSED** sign on the door to be reversed, listening for the little click that announces the door is now unlocked. Because I am old, I am often deferred to, urged to go in first, but no matter what the order, each of us courteously holds the door open for the person behind us. We are imbued with the kind of civility appropriate to a company of adventure-seekers about to enter a realm of unlimited possibilities.

Invariably, I stop first at the shelves of new non-fiction books. When looking at the array of volumes dealing with the real world, I immediately begin to have a surreal experience. There is no way for my brain to accommodate in any conventional way the subject matter that ranges from how to raise a puppy or get a divorce or make wise investments, to how to read tarot cards and/or travel in outer space. My selections are mostly random, and may deal with people and matters that have held no previous interest for me. These serendipitous choices have amazed, horrified, delighted, flabbergasted, and educated me. I am rarely disappointed.

Next, I browse in the new fiction section, seeking a best-seller recommended by a friend. I consider eye-catching titles, examine dust jacket illustrations, check the reviewers' comments, read brief author bios, and eyeball the author's picture. With the same kind of discrimination as a candy-lover picking his favorite caramels out of a box of chocolates, I make my selection and drop another couple of volumes into my book bag.

Then I remember that the reason I came to the library in the first place was to locate a copy of Don Marquis' *The Adventures of Archy and Mehitebel*, published in 1925. This is one of the choices my reading group has made. When I cannot find it among the Ms on the fiction shelves, the librarian locates it for me in the literature section. We laugh together as we look at the illustration on the cover of the old volume, and she comments that it has been years since she's thought about that particular book. She obligingly scans the computer to see if the County

Library system has other holdings by the same author. My book bag now bulges with as heavy a load as I can carry.

While my books are being processed, I look about me and am surprised to see that now there are many more of us in the library than the small flock of early birds I came in with. All of the computers are busy, their users staring into them with the hunched fixity peculiar to the technologically involved. A man and woman are discussing possible selections from the video section. A lone man is looking over the collection of audio books. Several people are seated at the reading tables with outspread newspapers or a stack of magazines. A woman is gathering up pages from the copying machine.

I realize that I am standing in the midst of marvels. I am amazed by the bustle and vigor of this library, so seemingly unrelated to my home town's small Carnegie Library, the one I first entered eighty years ago. That was a hushed and hallowed place which I humbly loved, a place where I tip-toed up to the librarian's desk to check out the Raggedy Ann books I adored. Going to that library was not too different from going to church, and indeed I did learn to worship there: I developed a lifelong reverence for books.

The library of my old age is a lively place which I enter without my childhood humility but still with the same joyful anticipation of long ago. The old reverence lingers, too, and I carry away my bag full of books with a feeling of exaltation.

Lucille K. Lovestedt is a retired speech pathologist, 85 years old, living in Grass Valley

Only the Beginning

CHRISTINE IRVING

Li·brar·y (li'brer·ē)

1. **Free** — may be used by or is open to all. As a child, I received books only at birthdays and Christmas. My allowance was twenty-five cents a week, but growing up I read at least a book a day. Without free access to a free library I wouldn't be half the person I am now.

2. **Sanctuary** — a sacred holy place. A place of refuge, quiet and repose. No shouting allowed. Calm haven of approval. Libraries love children who love to read. Even some mothers like children who like to read. My mother esteemed literacy. She didn't mind our weekly trips to the library—maybe they were as great a relief to her as to me. The library took the fight out of both of us and gave us common ground. I checked out stacks of books every week; always the limit. Each book retained the library's aura. When I opened a book and that faint library smell wafted out of the pages, my troubles fell away and I stepped over a sacred threshold and disappeared. Reading, I was lost to my family—I couldn't see them or hear them.

3. **Lifeline** — assistance at a critical time. If not for the library I would have drowned in a sea of self-doubt. My ideas seemed so different, so at odds with the views of those around me. The first time I read the story of the Ugly Duckling I wept. I finished it, though, and went on to read all of Hans Christian Anderson's stories. His dark world of wounded children nurtured only by brief flickers of color and beauty from un-peopled nature told my lonely heart that it did not dwell in isolation. Other children suffered in the same way. I found other validations and confirmations in the library as well as guidelines for living, which serve me to this day. Piglet and Ratty, Sancho Panza and Ralph Waldo Emerson taught me how to be a friend. Mary Poppins confirmed that there was more to the world than meets the eye. The Hundred Acre Wood showed me how community accommodates diversity. All the wildly eccentric characters I loved so dearly from Toad to Ben Franklin said it was okay to be different. An array of heroines from Alice to Caddie Woodlawn to Dido Twite convinced me, in spite of much evidence to the contrary, that it was good to be a girl.

4. **Time machine** — vehicle for transporting its passenger backward and forward in time. What adventures! Each trip to the library

brought new destinations: Cleopatra's boudoir, a Neolithic cave, The Battle of Hastings, Regency England. I crossed the Atlantic half a dozen times with Columbus, Leif Erickson, Brendan the Monk, Bluebeard, Josephine Bonaparte, and most recently a fleet of Chinese sailing vessels. I read all the Signature Series biographies. I gobbled up historical romances. I read a thousand mysteries set in medieval China, ancient Egypt, Victorian London, post-war Italy before I filled in the gaps with more serious history. The library's time machine ran forward as well as backward, carrying me from Mars and Venus out into the Ring Worlds, through the vast reaches of the Federation and on towards Earthsea and Dune and a hundred other planets scattered throughout the galaxies. Neverland was only the beginning.

5. **Continuity**— the state or quality of being continuous. My whole life has been spent in motion. As a child I moved from place to place, school to school, home to home. Wherever we went there was always a library. I married a man whose jobs took us all over the globe—wherever we went there was always some kind of a library. One of my favorites was the old two-story stone building in Marysville, California. We used to spend the summers on my grandmother's peach ranch ten miles out of town. It was always hot, hot, hot—the library was a haven of coolness and contained a complete collection of Gene Stratton Porter, which I reread every summer in their entirety. All libraries smell the same; they have the same rules, share the same system of organization. It's like coming home. The library has been a bulwark in my life, a companion in every kind of circumstance, it has seen me through crisis, pulled me out of depression, supported my studies, entertained my children, and brought me to a fullness of life and memory for which I am eternally grateful. I cannot do without my library.

Nevada City resident Christine Irving is the author of To Be a Singer of Tales

My Constant Companions

NANCY WILLIAMS

ONE day, not so long ago, I decided that it was time to clean out my wallet, a chore that I usually avoid because I'm a packrat by nature, and it is difficult for me to decide what to keep and what to discard. Besides, the grocery clerk's long, red fingernail tapping on the counter while I searched for my "rewards card" was getting on my nerves. So, settling down at the kitchen table one evening, I emptied the contents of the wallet on to it. Wow, I thought, this may take a bit longer than I expected, so I poured myself a nice glass of cold white wine and set it on the table, too.

As I sorted through the stuff, I found some interesting items, including five credit cards (one had expired two years ago); six photographs of my children, who, at first, I mistook for my grandchildren; a checkbook and check register with the last entry posted over a month ago (this didn't bother me very much, since I also found several grocery bills tucked into the change purse of the wallet); three other "rewards" from markets I never go to; and eight library cards.

Eight library cards! Well, I am a reader, but really! Spreading the cards on the table in date order, I saw that I could track my whereabouts for the last thirty-five years, give or take a year or two. Leaning back and sipping my wine I realized that one of the first things on my "to do" list when I move to a new home is to visit the local library. The cards themselves brought me memories of times past, mostly good, sometimes not.

Big or small, card-catalogued or computerized, as soon as I step through library doors, I feel at home. I don't know why, but libraries are personal to me; and I like to think that they have been put together just for my enjoyment. I really appreciate walking down the quiet aisles and recognizing books that have been my constant companions over the years, or, picking out a new author's contribution, hoping I can add the author to my favorites' list.

So, back into the wallet went the cards, because, even though I don't expect to be moving anytime soon, one never knows; and it's very possible that I already have a card from one of those eight towns. Also, you never know, someday someone might ask me what I was doing in such and such a town in such and such a year, and I'll just flip open my wallet and pull out a card!

Nancy Williams lives in Penn Valley

The Library Is Closed

RAY HADLEY

I love the library best when it's closed,
in a small town, one block off the main drag.

Who can remember the hours?
10 to 4 on Tuesday and Thursday, 9 to 5
Friday and Saturday, closed
Mondays and Sunday.

Dorianne Laux once admitted
she stole a copy of *A Tree Grows in Brooklyn*
then used it in a poem as I use
her poem in my poem now.

Somewhere an eighth grade girl worries
that her book, *To Kill a Mockingbird*,
is overdue. She calculates the fine
and deducts it from her allowance.

There's probably a waiting list
for J. K. Rowling's
Harry Potter and the Goblet of Fire,
but none for the poetry that should be here,
no waiting list for Congreve's
The Way of the World.

We cup our hand to the window
trying to see what's inside,
row after row.

It's all part of Borges' labyrinth

The lights are on tonight in every library,
a necklace of lights alongside Highway 80,
from Roseville to Sparks, Nevada

Poet Ray Hadley lives in South Lake Tahoe

The Princesses of the Roseville Library

ROSE NIETO

I AM a few steps away from the swings where my two sons, Adrian and Paul, five and two years old respectively, push themselves very hard to touch the sky with their sneakers' tips. I am trying to steal a few sun rays away from the big Sequoia that shades the playground. The children seem not to notice the ending of the winter afternoon in Royer Park. I inform them that after five minutes we are going to go to the library. They both ask why. I feel chilly and it's too early for dinner. I think for a minute and answer, "to borrow some books."

We head toward the children's section inside the library. I sit on a little sofa while the kids dig out books from a big plastic basket. In the center of the room there is a tripod holding a square covered with fabric, where you can attach the characters of stories, animals, houses, and trees also made of cloth. The walls facing the library's main room are tall glass dividers with sliding doors. The walls facing the street are decorated with glossy paper pretending to be leaves where leopards, panthers and snakes hide. Tall palm trees house parrots, doves, and toucans. I recognize the monkey, Curious George, who shows up repeatedly in this improvised jungle. Hanging paper vines stretch down over the horizontal window panes. These last ones filter the dim sunlight between the outer walls and the ceiling.

I count twenty-two little mats on the Berber carpet for tomorrow's story time. A few days ago Paul glued his nose to the glass door, trying to follow the librarian's story; we couldn't get in because we hadn't signed up in advance. The place retains so many remnants of its inhabitants—the crooked giraffes on the tripod, puffed-bean boxes, one little book here and there—that I feel I am intruding in Toddler Land. Paul asks me to read a book he picked from the basket. He likes it because it has a huge colorful dragon. It talks about a paper-bag princess who figures out at the end that although the prince is very well dressed, he is a bum at heart. In my time, the princess never had a meaningful conversation with the prince to know if they would get along in the future. This new princess is very assertive. The book is ripped and put together with tape, but I decide to take it home to study it deeply with the children.

We read more stories. In one of them, a little boy learns to play after the television set breaks. I almost cry over another story, one where the mother takes care of her son all her life and the son takes care of her when she gets old. After a while they don't bring me more books to read. They are building a new story on the fabric square, helped by two little long-haired princesses who have also put aside their books. Now I am getting hungry, but Adrian and Paul don't want to go home.

Rose Nieto lives in Roseville

My Library Home

JOHN CHURCH

I GREW up traveling with my salesman father through the Intermountain states from Montana and Idaho to Arizona and New Mexico. He wanted to have his family of my mother, sister Rie, and me with him. We would be in a community from three days to occasionally three weeks.

We came to know people in different places where we would visit every year—in Phoenix, for instance, we would celebrate Christmas. There John Tovrea had told my sister and me the story of a scary movie he had seen, when he asked me,

"Where *is* your home?"

After thinking about this for a few minutes, I thought of my two homes. One that was always there for me was our car, in which we carried all of our possessions. I said, "Our car."

And then I added enthusiastically, "And the Public Library!"

In each town we found the library—the same one we had visited the year before. Inside were the rows of bookshelves with enticing stories and books that answered questions that had raised my curiosity and others that opened up new vistas.

I'll paint a word picture for you of a typical day. We were in Butte, Montana, a copper-mining town built on the top of hills which were honeycombed with tunnels underneath. On the surface, sidewalks, railings, and even trees in this overall gray city were covered with soot from smelters nearby. We started the day with our ex-teacher mother guiding us through our lessons with books we had purchased a few weeks earlier at the Schools Supply store in Great Falls. For reading we devoured books we had borrowed the previous day from the Butte Carnegie Free Public Library. We exercised walking steep hills topped by the scaffolding above mine shafts where ore had in earlier days been hauled up from far below. Our pace hastened as we came nearer to the library.

Often the library had a capitol-like dome, but here we climbed down steps to enter and leave the bleakness of the city. Inside we were greeted by a busy but friendly lady librarian who remembered us from year to year. She trusted us even though we were transients and even gave us library cards.

After a few years of devoting myself to fairy tales like those of the

Brothers Grimm and then the adventures of Dr. Doolittle, I came in asking for history books. Having read Hilyer's *Child's History of the World*, I wanted more. For a period of time I gained a feeling for the pre-Revolutionary era, reading about early frontier men with Altsheller's *Runners of the Woods*. And thanks to the rich collection in the library I was able to move on through history with, for instance, his *Guns of Shiloh*.

On this day I curled up with my book from the history section and was lost in sensing the smoke and confusion and pain of the Civil War. When I came to the word "amputated" I asked the librarian nearby for a definition, which she showed me how to find in a dictionary. I returned to the book and soon found myself identifying with a soldier who had many rich qualities and a lot to live for.

In each library I felt a warm pleasure in just being there within the book atmosphere of the library with the caring librarian. All too soon my mother gathered Rie and me up to go to lunch, but we each departed with a new book and a new set of thoughts in our hands. In a few days we left Butte. In each town we came to—Idaho Falls, Twin Falls, Ogden, Salt Lake, and so on—we looked forward to our visits to our library home that we could always depend on for new realms in books.

As we left Butte in our car, we felt in spirit the joy of being "on the road again," which we chimed out in unison as we looked at the road ahead, knowing we would soon be in another library with books, a librarian, and a peaceful place to read.

John G. Church, Ph.D., a retired librarian, resides in Nevada City, and produces and hosts an education program on NCTV

John Church and his sister *carefully* read books from the Ketchum, Idaho, store-front library in the pool, while their mother looks on.

Imagine That You Can't Read

ALAN ARCHER

FOR a moment, close your eyes and imagine that you never learned to read. How would life be different for you? Your life would not resemble the way it is right now. It would be different in ways that have a huge impact on who and what you are, and in small, subtle ways that eat away at you every day.

To begin with, your education would be almost nil. Your speaking vocabulary would be very limited; your spelling and grammar unintelligible; you would have no ability to write.

The reading and completion of even simple forms and documents is beyond your ability. Applying for a job becomes a major obstacle to your survival. The chances of getting a job with good pay and benefits is remote. Newspapers, magazines, and books make no sense to you other than what you can glean from the pictures. There is no such thing as "reading for pleasure."

Maps, street signs, advertising and business signs are of no use to you in your travels; you must rely on asking directions and being able to remember them. Just like you must be able to remember what the pharmacist tells you about the RX directions, or your new boss explains about the details of a new job, or a fellow employee telling you what the bulletin board posting says, or relatives and friends telling you about a tasty recipe you should prepare. Everything hinges on your ability to remember.

If you couldn't read, it is unlikely you would enjoy your current level of economic success, nor would you have met and married your current spouse. Neither would you be held in high esteem in the eyes of others. Starting in elementary school other students ridiculed you for being unable to read. It hasn't gotten any better over the years. Your self-esteem has always been low, and you have never been confident in your ability to take on new challenges. Relationships with others have been difficult because you are not conversant on many topics, and your understanding of issues is very limited. You do not vote because the issues are so confusing and you fear the embarrassment of not being able to go to the polls and complete the process. The odds are very strong that you are intimately familiar with unemployment lines, social welfare lines, and that you have a criminal record.

You get the picture. Close your eyes for a few more moments and keep imagining. It keeps on getting worse. Library literacy programs help people learn to read by offering free, confidential, one-on-one tutoring. This is life changing!

Alan Archer of Grass Valley is the Literacy Coordinator for Nevada County Library

A Ticket to Anywhere

JEANIE HARRIS

As a child, I wanted to read more than anything. At three, I'd hold a book and pretend to read out loud. I knew the little black squiggles on the page *meant* something, and I yearned to be one of those who knew that secret code.

On a hot summer day when I was six years old, I held my mother's hand and walked into the Campbell library. Perhaps she was at her wit's end with a bored, fidgety child and a nonexistent entertainment budget.

But that day opened the world for me. I remember the cool, the quiet, the tall shelves, and the smell of books. The place felt reverent —almost like church.

Mrs. Booth, the librarian, smiled over the counter. "So, you're going to get your very own library card today," she said.

I'd never felt so proud as when I carefully printed my name and then roamed the aisles. The shelves in the children's section were shorter and less intimidating. I plopped on the floor cross-legged to scan the colorful offerings. By now I'd learned to read and could decipher those black squiggles into words.

We made many treks to the library that summer. I'd slide my library card across the counter to Mrs. Booth and walk out with a big grin and an armful of books. Though we didn't have a vacation, I went many places—to magical lands with dragons and princes, to the moon, a mysterious cave, and even back in time! I learned the names of the orange and black butterflies that flitted about our yard. And I had a new best friend named Ramona—courtesy of Beverly Cleary.

Later I experienced 19th century England through the eyes of a horse while reading my favorite book, *Black Beauty*. I cried when his cruel master beat him. As I got older, I rode my bike to the library, and books filled the basket attached to the handlebars.

I discovered Edgar Rice Burroughs and swung through the trees with Tarzan. I went to Mars and Pellucidar—the center of the Earth. I traveled across the Pacific on a raft named Kon-Tiki with fellow Norwegian, Thor Heyerdahl.

One day I found out that if our local library didn't have the exact book I wanted, Mrs. Booth would order it from another branch. Just for me! A few days later we got a phone call that "my" book had arrived.

Jumping on my bike, I raced to the library, bending over to go faster, with the breeze blowing my ponytail behind me.

I stood at the library doors and realized that the rumpled library card in my back pocket was a free ticket to *anywhere*. I could go anywhere in this world, or any other world, backward or forward in time, to the microscopic world of molecules, or into the vastness of space. I realized that I could find out or learn anything that I wanted—and all for free. It was a powerful epiphany.

Later, I wallowed in teen angst by reading the poetry of Sylvia Plath. Thankfully, that phase didn't last long. The library also became a respectable place to meet cute boys. Mrs. Booth's curly brown hair was turning silver and she grew a bit plumper every year. But her warm smile never wavered and she didn't mind the gaggle of teenagers, as long as we stayed reasonably quiet.

As an adult, the library became my refuge once again. And after I had my own daughter, the library was a cool oasis on a blistering summer day with a bored, fidgety child and a nonexistent entertainment budget. Now my daughter chose her own books and we'd cuddle in bed at night—each transported to a world of our choosing.

The library is like a faithful friend, a comfortable pair of shoes, or that old denim jacket that's molded itself to your shape over the years. Though libraries have changed with the times and now offer much more than just books, they're still a limitless storehouse of human knowledge and imagination. With a library card, you can learn anything.

Recently, I saw a little girl walking out of the library with her mother, carrying a stack of picture books she could barely see over. I couldn't help smiling, her joy was contagious and all too familiar. That lucky little girl has a ticket to anywhere.

Jeanie Harris is a writer living in Meadow Vista

San Miguel de Allende, 2000

MARK WILSON

Respite from the diesel, dust, and noise
of the narrow cobbled Mexican street,
the familiar bookcases and smells
of paper, glue, and cardboard
inside the *biblioteca publica*

Sitting in the open courtyard,
among fragrant flowers and cool,
cracked, hand-painted tiles,
unfamiliar birds crisscross the sky,
and scrawny cats mingle with us,
as four-year-old Emma
discovers bilingualism
between the covers of
¿Dónde Está Wally?

Mark Wilson lives in Grass Valley

Fair Haven Found

PAMELA BIERY

I REMEMBER coming early sometimes on Saturdays and climbing the broad stonewalls that lined the staircase, a wide stone handrail set with a graded peak, making sliding down to the end-cap buttress almost impossible. The end-cap itself was carved into a peak, too—with four adjoining points, making it uncomfortable to perch and play on. So the steps of the Fairhaven Public Library in Bellingham, Washington, maintained a sense of dignity, warding off at least some of the more aggressive tactics children, left waiting for a ride or a locked door to open, resort to. A big square, solid building of grey, split-block sandstone. Windows with wooden frames finished with green enamel paint. Above the big first-storey windows are smaller second-storey windows, divided into quadrangles, like little stars. The building stood square, solid and welcoming, in a stoic sort of way—at least in my mind's eye today. Fairhaven Library seemed sterner to me as a child, though.

Shelves lined with books below the low window were within my easy reach. Sitting on the floor with my knees together and legs turned out looking at pictures and flipping pages, wandering far away in stories. There never was a thought of a book as a luxury—a book was a basic right to go and obtain, provided a few minor disciplines were followed, like using your "library voice" and returning borrowed books on time. By the age of eight, I could walk to the library on my own, and use the card file to find special books, or ask the librarian for help. Many fascinating characters came into my life while reading *Blueberries for Sal, Ferdinand the Bull*, following Ping and his trip on the Yangtze River, Officer McCloskey and his duckling wards. Later came Hans Brinker, Harriet the Spy, Ramona and other fabulous friends. There was always something wonderful, almost divine, about being able to spread so many books out around me and choose three or four to take home each visit.

Maybe this is why, years later when my middle-grade school peers exploded into fragmented adolescence, the school library became a familiar place. Our librarian, Mrs. Richardson, was a very hip young adult. She became my friend, taught me how to sort, catalog, and shared new books with me. Visiting University District bookstores with Marianne Richardson became a preferred pastime. Not unlike childhood Saturdays, the school library provided respite and retreat.

For long periods, I drifted away from libraries, only to find myself back, looking for some knowledge, wanting to discover some fact, or find a poem waiting for me. This attitude no doubt grew up in me alongside the presence of libraries, unlocking ideas and opportunities even when my pockets were empty and my luck seemed down.

Have you ever considered longingly the smell peculiar to musty pages, or fresh ink, or the creak of a new binding on its first opening? There is excitement in a chance encounter with an eye-catching book, a stray title miscatalogued, or the book left on a table that invites you into its pages. Some of my favorite books are those I never intended to read. Libraries bring orphaned ideas and strange pages home to my mind.

Up the stone stairs, a big brass-framed door with a solid brass latch and matching brass push-plates waited to open the world of ideas to me. It was a giant door for a child, worth pushing open and walking through.

Pamela Biery runs a public relations firm in Nevada County and is a member of Sierra Writers

The Library

LOUIS B. JONES

FOR some reason, I always find myself entering by the far-right door, the heavy, hard-to-open door for the physically challenged, prying my way into the foyer by elbow and shoulder, neglecting the hydraulic opening system. (Why is every library foyer so sad, the no-man's-land of floor tiles, the unvisited displays in vitrines, the mournful drinking fountain, the rack of pamphlets?) I'm only here to drop a few books in the square slot at the return counter, but here's my friend's newly-published book of poetry, kindly propped up in display at the checkout desk. It's something they do here, at this library, because he happens to live in the neighborhood. He's a local boy done well. I'm proud to know the man, he's a startling poet, but even more, I've been startled and changed by his writing. In fifty years, he has changed a lot of people's minds about important things. I find he's someone I think of often, miscellaneously. Though I don't know him well and though I never visit him across the river, yet he's one of those remote people I measure myself by.

Just this morning I was standing on a chair outside my backdoor swatting at carpenter bees with a badminton racquet, thinking: How would *he* combat carpenter bees? Because he's a true card-carrying follower of the Dharma, might he possibly just coexist with the things? And let his house fall to powder in those tiny mandibles of theirs that make audible crunches in the night as they carve out their galleries in the wood? No, he was always a country boy, it's likely he grew up with the redneck's unsentimentality, or then the Zen priest's unsentimentality, at least in regard to certain sentient beings. And those black shiny bees, they are my nemesis. Big as marbles. They survive all poisons. They levitate with unmistakable menace, motionless in my cross-eyed vision, sizing me up. The way they linger, I see their contempt for me. They're big. Each one looks like it could weigh a quarter-ounce. I've seen this happen: in a single midsummer night, these small round obsidian-shiny people chewed one gaping mouth into my north eave, sweet old twice-salvaged lumber from the nineteenth century, now in its third incarnation.

Now, though, I've discovered the children's badminton racquet. I can hit that hovering shiny thing just at the moment it's pausing to focus on me, with such a satisfying thwack, I can feel through the shaft of the racquet how massive is its body, and then the corpse lifts, in a short limp arc to land in a spot where I can stomp it, for good measure. I bet, I *bet*, that Buddhist out there on the Ridge does the very same thing. He's lived here forty years: he knows about carpenter bees, and over forty years he will have tried all the other remedies, none of which work. He mentioned once, whenever we get a heavy wet snowfall in these mountains, he has to go outside in the night with a twenty-foot length of iron pipe, to bang on the Japanese maples that don't belong at this elevation, to knock the snow off the branches and save them from snapping off. The point is, I'd developed the exact same technique myself, even to the length of old pipe, and I rather prized remote men's having similar solutions to problems, oh, problems. One thinks of him all the more lately: I wonder, rather stupidly, if being an accomplished, serious, Buddhist makes the finality thing any different, and then I think, *Oh, probably not*.

In the matter of saying goodbye, Buddhism isn't going to be any help, any more than anything helps, because nothing helps, isn't it the First Noble Truth? Plenty of us around these canyons think of him often, maybe daily, and wish there were such a thing as consolation. The new book of poems mentions nothing of grief. He always did, unfashionably, seem to think poetry isn't a place for emotional display. Part of a book's job is to keep its place on the library shelf, in this heavenly mausoleum in the hum of fluorescence, and not get culled at springtime, segregated on the wheeled metal gurney, and sold for a quarter on tables outside in the sunshine. A writer who has a book or two in most libraries will still sometimes, in fame's gloom, furtively, visit the rear stacks to check. Of course I've read the new poetry collection, but yet I find myself here sitting in a hard chair by the reference-catalogue computers, Harpo and Groucho and Zeppo, revisiting everything, until at last the world calls again, that great roaring stadium at our back, and I replace the book in its propped stand by the check-out counter, as a gift for someone else, someone who doesn't know about it yet. Out through the Know-Go alarm system detection gate; through the sad narthex, every library's foyer is always so eternally forbidding, so mysterious, such a zone of passage-between-worlds, a transition that is, in some way, impossible.

Headed home again in sunshine, my eyesight pixilated by a visit to a public library, I have a thought. Those carpenter bees represent a mean form of incarnation. Somewhere just above the hell of Hungry Ghosts. A carpenter bee, what does *it* see, when through its compound eye it looks out at the world? It sees only diagrammatic transparencies, enlivened in places only by clots of discontentment. That bee will have many lives to traverse before it may attain the level of existence of a fiction writer, a comparatively refined exalted creature, standing on a chair, badminton racquet poised in patience and cunning.

When I whack one, I'm batting it straight out into the infinite worlds, the billions of incarnations, easily detonating the chain-reaction of sangsara, of suffering, by fission causing a trillion lives-to-come, all the swarms of sentient beings unredeemed in grief. This is my dharma, me with this racquet from Big Five. So I have the same thought as that scientist Oppenheimer at Los Alamos, the remorseful one on the scene, who spoke aloud a line of the *Baghvad Gita* at the moment when he saw, from the bunker, his new fireball leap in the desert: "I am become Death, Destroyer of Worlds." Down the four shallow steps outside the library. Past the bronze statue of the little girl reading. Off the curb. The parking lot, the sunshine. No consolation out here.

Louis B. Jones of Nevada City is the author of three novels:
Ordinary Money, Particles and Luck, *and* California's Over

The Phantom of the Library

SOUMITRO SEN

I saw him first at the National Library in Calcutta in mid-summer.
Leaving the company of others—shiny black heads, studiously combed, quaintly hair-oiled—
He chose to sit in a shadowy, stuffy corner,
Far away from the old, torpid fans suspended
With long grimy poles from the high, cobwebbed ceiling.
He read as if there was no tomorrow, looking up occasionally,
Staring out of the window, murmuring something to himself with a frown,
While the afternoon winds quietly singed the parks in the midst of town.
But once, when I passed him by, and peered over his shoulder,
I noticed the tome before him, was placed upside down.
He turned around
And following my gaze, with a broad smile, said,
"This is the way to know a world that's spinning on its head."

A few months later, I met him again,
When the dark-grey monsoon clouds
Swept over the white-washed colonial mansion,
And the verdant, rain-washed lawn.
He sat with Plato on his lap, looking forlorn
And uprooted grass from the rain-scented soil.
But when I left the long driveway from the gate to the library,
And walked up to him through the slush,
He grinned and said to me,
"This is the way to truly understand
The transience of pain,
From the dead grass on your hand."
After that, I saw him off and on
Sometimes in the plush, maroon-carpeted library of the American Embassy,
Perusing Twain, Whitman or Gunn.
In the British Council Library amidst grey, metal bookshelves
Skimming lines from Chaucer, Keats or Donne.
Sometimes in the guise of an English major,

At times, with the face of a musty professor,
He would appear, and looking at me,
Smile knowingly.
And once when I asked what he's looking for,
He replied, "Well? ... Immortality."

Then for years, I didn't see him anymore.
In the meantime, I moved to America,
Went to grad school.
Learned precepts by rote,
Trained thoughts to evolve by the rule.

One April evening, he turned up in Tennessee,
At the end of an aisle in the Vanderbilt Library,
Where I was rummaging for a reference book,
Right in the middle of a perfect vacation.
With a bright contented smile he stood—
Brown, disheveled head, beaming face.
And as if to do me good,
He beckoned and said,
"This is the wrong place
To search for immortality."
"Where did you find it then?" I asked eagerly.

He led me at once to the sidewalks,
And turned me to the traffic rushing by.
People driving homewards at the end of day,
A tired glimmer of hope in every eye.
And just life, swarming all around—
Nameless faces, aimless footsteps, urban sounds.
Just life and life alone ... relentlessly surviving.
With every fall, a more-persistent striving ...
Every second when one hope is dead
Another dream is born.
I smiled and turned to thank him,
But my old friend, he was gone.

Soumitro Sen is a feature writer and education reporter for **The Union**

Before and After

ROSANNE STRATIGAKES

Pre-brain-tumor surgery 1951–2003:

I have always loved the library!

Growing up in the Detroit area, experiencing the beauty of the Santa Barbara Library, seeing the Palmdale Library grow, and using the Nevada County Libraries, I truly see how they have added value to my life. I loved taking my young children to the library. They instilled relaxed feelings in me and I would learn fast. I also learned where the restrooms were located!

Post-brain-tumor surgery 2003–present:

WOW! I still love and use the library.

I appreciate using the online services. At this point it is the only truly functional handicapped door in town that I know of. The blue handicapped parking spots are usually open. Last year I practiced going to the bathroom by myself there (my husband would rather assist me in a single-stall facility—understandably).

My husband has gotten turned on to the library by taking me every Thursday night. He even has gotten to know a wonderful librarian and they talk books. He reads to me in the morning, on the porch in summer and by the fire in winter. With the help of my friends, I still take out children's picture books and leave them lying around the front room. Somehow they are rearranged. I've also used the library as a venue to relearn to walk. Progressing from wheelchair to walker to cane, it is wonderfully accessible. I see friends there and sometimes forget to laugh softly.

I love the library and always have a book with me, only now I make sure it is on the walker-chair so I don't have to take extra steps to get it.

Rosanne Stratigakes lives in Grass Valley

The Need to Know More

JEFF ACKERMAN

WHEN he was five years old and in kindergarten, my son Luke's teacher met with us to say she could no longer keep him in her classroom.

"He won't stop when I blow my whistle," she said. "He just keeps on reading his book and won't put it down. I can't have every kid doing his own thing or there would be total chaos."

"Is that it?" I asked, trying to understand why my son was being reprimanded for reading a book.

"No it isn't," the teacher said, her voice turning to a whisper. "He can't count from one to ten."

"Really?" I replied. "Hey, Luke," I said, turning toward my son, who was fiddling with something on the other side of the crowded classroom. "Count from one to ten."

Luke proceeded to count from one to ten without looking up.

"See?" I said to the surprised and blushing teacher. "Luke. How come you didn't count to ten when she asked you to?"

"Because I didn't want to," he said, as if the answer was obvious.

It's not every day a son gets kicked out of kindergarten, so we knew there was something special about Luke. He'd always been a quiet boy, who had difficulty communicating. His sister, 13 months his senior, always did the talking for him.

"Are you hungry?" I asked him.

"No. He's not," his sister would reply.

We were advised to take Luke to a neurologist for an examination. It quickly determined that he was autistic, or at least suffering from what was called Asparger's Syndrome, a high-functioning form of autism. I use the term "suffering" loosely, because Luke, who is 13 today, doesn't seem to be suffering at all. Luke's "disease" has been a gift. Fixation is a symptom of autism and Luke is fixated on learning. When he is interested in something he will study it for months and months. When he was five he could identify the flag of any country in the world and most all of their capitals.

By the time he was six he knew every rivet on the Titanic and built a couple of 3-D puzzles. Skyscrapers were next, then natural disasters and anatomy (he gave his mother a video on melanoma when he was seven because he saw a spot on her back and he wanted to make sure it wasn't serious.)

The local library and bookstores became Luke's personal theme parks. We would head for the library every Saturday for three to four hours. Over time, Luke got to know all of the library employees and they adored him.

We would check out as many books as they would allow and Luke would pore over each and every one of them. With the help of a Librarian Assistant, Luke quickly learned how to use the Dewey Decimal Classification System, combining his growing computer skills to allow for a much more rapid search for knowledge. And all the while I used the opportunity to learn right along with my son. At first I was consumed with self-pity. I'd always imagined coaching Little League for my son's team. Maybe even a basketball team or two. But there we were, on a summer Saturday, looking up information on the Seven Ancient Wonders of The World because Luke just had to know more.

Sadly, the World Wide Web has replaced much of Luke's library time. He learned to Google very early in life, and even DSL is no match as he works several windows simultaneously from the comfort of his own bedroom.

We'll spend time at Barnes & Noble, or perhaps at some used bookstore from time to time, but our library days are rare. Yet I will never forget those days ... those many, many days ... whispering with my son down some lonely library aisle, his eyes dancing from page to page, his mind whirling to digest every last word, photo, or illustration. Nor will I forget those many wonderful library employees and volunteers, who understood and nurtured my son's love for books.

Jeff Ackerman is the Publisher of The Union

With the In-Crowd of Readers

GAGE McKINNEY

A SPEECH impediment left me withdrawn as a child and made me decidedly unpopular as a boy. This lifted miraculously when I got to junior high where I became an athlete, president of my class, and popular. At an age when peers matter so much, I had the approval of the stylish clique, the socially attractive girls and boys. Not wanting to jeopardize this, I kept to myself a bookishness I had developed in lonelier years and the fact that I had enrolled in librarianship. This class taught us how to use a library and acquainted us with the rudimentary work like shelving and cataloging books, or for the advanced, repairing them. On account of the pleasure of being with books, and the new books I discovered while shelving, it became my favorite class. To extend my pleasure and please the teacher (who liked me as everyone seemed to then), I volunteered after school, shelving books or staffing the circulation desk on the days I wasn't playing sports.

My fashionable friends began wondering where I was in the afternoon. When they tracked me to the library, I expected my status to drop like a book in the return chute. To my surprise, I was credited with originality and my status increased. To the librarian's surprise, the most fashionable kids on campus started coming to the library regularly after school, sharing tables with kids who carried brief cases or musical instruments and were known to be unfashionably studious. The following term some of my friends enrolled in librarianship.

I suspected my popularity would be fleeting (and it was). Having no conviction in my own magnetism, I never thought that I had much to do with my friends becoming enthusiastic patrons of the library. Once I began meeting them there, I discovered they each had their own relationship with books, their own favorites and range of particular interests (referenced in my mind at that time as Dewey Decimal numbers). Reading and stories had shaped them as they had shaped me. The books they had read with their parents or siblings were part of their family life. The books they discovered for themselves, or read on the librarian's recommendation, became part of their personal histories. In green youth my friends and I discovered an unexpected bond through books.

I read once of a Nova Scotia fisherman who became a voracious reader in middle age. One season, when fishing was so scant that it didn't pay to untie the boats, he was inspired by his children in college to begin serious reading. He started with a shelf of great books, including history and Shakespeare, and then moved on to the great novelists. By the time the fishing fleet sailed again, he had begun studying philosophy. He died later in an Atlantic storm.

Most of us came to reading more conventionally, as I did. I loved stories at bedtime and I learned through books of pictures and rhymes. In my case I had the added advantage of following my older brother through the pages of Alexandre Dumas and other writers. Sometimes on Sunday afternoons I accompanied my father to the public library.

Reading, books, and libraries are among the strongest checks on the atomizing pull of our times. Libraries are the center of communities that are formed, as philosopher Josiah Royce described it, by individuals seeking their own fulfillment. We come to the library as individual readers and coalesce into a community of learning. We might find almost anyone beside us there because membership merely requires that we roam the stacks, concentrate on a page at a time, and possess a card that costs nothing or next to nothing.

This communal experience deepens when at one time or another you pick up a book that afterwards you can't forget, a book that strikes you as with a deep wound, so that you go on thinking and talking about it for years. Once that happens, you are inescapably bound with readers and librarians, the authors you've read, and the authors those authors read. Through the library you belong to the most fashionable clique I know, the society of students and explorers who share a quest for knowledge. This society you have joined endures through generations with a popularity that doesn't fade.

Gage McKinney is a member of the California Cornish Cousins who visits Nevada County regularly for his research

The Award
CHARLES ENTREKIN

BIRMINGHAM, Alabama. The summer of 1950, at age nine, I won an award for reading more books than anyone else in the Woodlawn Branch of the Birmingham Public Library. I still remember that award and the ceremony. The person who came in second place was an elderly lady. The library staff served grape Kool-Aid and sugar cookies. My mom and two of her sisters were there. They sat on folding chairs and applauded.

That summer marked a turning point in my life.

A shy boy, from a large family, I had failed the second grade and had been forced to go to summer school to make it up. In the second grade I sat in the back of the room and hid behind a large redheaded girl with big hair, and daydreamed. But in the third grade I encountered a teacher, Mrs. Holt, who read us stories. And oh what a treat that was. One day, much to my amazement, Mrs. Holt, who, for several days, had been reading to us from Jesse Stuart's *The Thread That Runs So True*, announced to our class that she wasn't going to read to us because we'd not been paying attention. I was so upset by her announcement that I rose up red-faced and addressed the class. Me, the shy boy who never talked, who had no friends, whose presence was simply overlooked, I stood up in front of the class and, knees shaking and voice cracking, begged and pleaded with my classmates to be quiet. Having stunned the teacher, my classmates, and myself, I then collapsed back in my chair. But Mrs. Holt continued on with that day's chapter.

That year Mrs. Holt and I became friends. And when she took our class on a walking excursion to the library for an educational tour, she helped me get a library card, and showed me how to check out C. S. Lewis's *The Horse and His Boy*. She said she thought I would enjoy visiting the library on my own.

I got all "E"s for "Excellent" that year.

And the following summer, one day, without telling anybody, because Mrs. Holt had suggested I might enjoy visiting the library on my own, I strapped on my roller skates and skated four miles across town to the Woodlawn Library, a two-room brick building at the back of a small park just off First Avenue South, to check out a book. And that day I discovered a whole shelf filled with horse and dog stories. From then on, every week, I went back to the library and checked out more. Until I had read them all. Every book they had about horses and dogs. I read all the stories I could get my hands on by Walter Farley: *The Black Stallion, The Island Stallion's Fury, Man O' War,* and lots more. I read Anna Sewall's *Black Beauty*. I read Jack London's *Call of the Wild* and *White Fang*. I read everything they had in that library about horses and dogs.

And then one day, much to my surprise, the library called my mom and told her I was going to win an award. So, Mom and two of her sisters, all dressed up and wearing wide-brimmed hats, surprised me by taking me to the Woodlawn Library. It was a day I would never forget. Suddenly, people noticed me.

Charles Entrekin is the author of many books of poetry and founded the Creative Writing Department at John F. Kennedy University, and the Berkeley Poets Workshop & Press

At Home in the Library

JANET ANN COLLINS

ONE night when I was six years old, my Daddy took me to get my first library card and afterwards, as I held his warm hand and we walked home past the redwoods in the park, he showed me the Big Dipper, sparkling in the dark sky overhead.

Soon afterwards he died.

My mom, working at a full time job, didn't have time to take me to the library, and it was over a year before I was old enough to go there alone after school. By then I had developed athsma and was teased by the kids in my class because I didn't have a father and couldn't join in active play.

The library soon became my refuge where I could escape into the hundreds of wonderful worlds in books. The things I read shaped my life, leading me to think, to enjoy the wonders of the world, and eventually to teach and write.

A few years ago I attended a high school reunion and was amazed that several of my elementary school classmates remembered me as being brave.

Me? Brave? I had been afraid of everything.

But then I was reminded of times when I had stood up for what was right. I realized that since that was how the protagonists acted in all the books I read, it had never occurred to me that there was any alternative.

The library was like a second home during my childhood. I would stay there for hours after school, reading and waiting for my mother to drive me home after she got off work because, while wheezing, it was difficult for me to climb the steep hill to our house.

The librarian taught me to shelve books, let me write my own number on the card to check them out, and always gave me the honor of being the very first to read any new children's books that were purchased.

After I married and became a mother, we bought a house almost across the street from another library. What a great location!

Because my widowed mother had worked away from home, I wanted to be there for my own daughter and began doing family daycare. Every week I'd take the children to preschool story time at the nearby library, and when we came back to the house they'd take turns pretending to be the librarian, saying sweetly, "Put your bottoms on the floor, dears." Then I'd read them the books they had chosen.

And, of course, even after my own children were grown and out of the nest, I would go to the library often to stock up on reading material.

Last summer my husband retired and we moved to Grass Valley. Although we had relatives in this beautiful area, it was difficult to leave the familiar home where we'd lived for so long. I had hardly begun unpacking when I went into town to apply for a library card. I was expecting a visit from my grandson, so I asked about preschool story time. To my horror, I was told they were without a children's librarian and there might not be any story times for months.

"I wish I could do it," I said.

Within minutes, Judy, the head librarian, was talking to me about volunteering, and before the day was over, I had agreed to do it, hoping to give back some of the joys libraries had given me.

And from that first Monday morning when the children gathered at story time to share the wonder of books, I felt completely at home in the library.

Janet Ann Collins lives in Grass Valley

Four Poems
JEAN McKEEN

First Library Visit
"My, little girl, you are certainly checking out a lot of books."

"I know, but I have to get started.
I'm going to read every book here."

Seventy years later
Countless libraries behind me
Goal not realized
Still checking out a lot of books.

My Life, A Moving Experience
Readers who move often
Don't buy books.
New town, vital question,
"Where's the library?"

On Returning Books to the Library
Go directly to return table.
Return books.
Resist lure of siren songs from stacks. Remember, he is double parked.

Apology to Booksellers
A friend recommends a good read.
My response, "Sounds great.
I'll check it out at the Library."

Jean McKeen, Nevada City, is a volunteer living history interpreter at the Empire Mine State Historic Park in Grass Valley

Part II. Keepers of the Culture

Library Thoughts

IVEN LOURIE

AND so—how magical were the Library and Librarians to me? I sat in the State Library in the capitol complex in Harrisburg, Pennsylvania, and gaped at three-storey-tall ceilings with baroque decoration; I inhaled the musty odor of archives there. Similarly awed, I sat in the reading room of the old neo-Gothic library at University of Chicago, glancing occasionally at the dark wood fluting from floor to arched ceilings and noting the monumental, architectural silence that enveloped us earnest scholars bent over our tomes. And yet, above all, the Wonder of Libraries was revived in me when I discovered, on the fourth floor of this as-if monastic edifice—the Poetry Library. This was housed in several cramped upper-storey rooms with ornately iron-worked windows looking far out over campus. It was accessed by a creaky elevator that ran up so slowly and offered such dusty air to breathe that you could not help but reflect on your mortality during the ascent. In these few dimly-lit rooms, hazy it seemed in sunshine or in fog, chill winter or sweet spring, were the mostly-slim volumes of all the poets of the English language, arranged alphabetically by author.

I made it my project to read from A to Z, A. R. Ammons and William Blake through W. B. Yeats and Louis Zukofsky. I don't recall how far I got—but I will never forget those archaic rooms, like something from a Borges story. Somehow I don't recall ever meeting other students there, only the Poetry Librarian, a demure woman with straight brown hair, horn-rimmed glasses of the scholar type, conservative woolen skirts and cotton blouses. She was of that indeterminable (to a college student) age, over 21 and somewhere under 40. We talked poets and poetry as she stared soberly at me through those thick lenses. When I learned that my Librarian was also a poet who had a slim volume in that very library, she rose in my esteem. However, to personal questions she demurred, suggesting only that poetry is a time-honored but never well-paid pursuit, and so she had settled on becoming an archivist of poetry.

I now mix her image not only with all those woman librarians who nurtured my hunger for adventure and fantasy as a child, but also with countless representations of The Muse. I can readily understand that Charles Olson dreamt the Gloucester, Massachusetts, librarian into his parents' and his own marriage bedroom in his poem "The Librarian," and that Joyce gave Stephen Dedalus a "Quaker librarian" as instigator of his great *Hamlet* lecture in the Dublin public library in *Ulysses*. These Librarians hold a place in our deepest childhood memories, be we artists, poets, or dreamers. They appear as fairy tale figures, etched in imagination. My Poetry Librarian is for me like another wraith who seemed eternal: the gaunt and grey-haired widow of a sculptor whose memory she enshrined by giving ghostly tours of their mansion-museum called Swananoa, off the Blue Ridge Parkway … but that is a story for another time and place.

Iven Lourie, Penn Valley, is a publisher and poet

Thank You Miss Groub

STEVE STANFIELD

As a child I loved to read. Oh, how I loved to read,
probably more than anything else in the entire world.
I read everything
the funny books in the rack
in back of Mrs. Burke's drugstore,
the stories on the cereal boxes,
my mother's magazines that came in the mail,
and I read books from the library
—as many as I could.

The Parrot Street Public Library
was only a mile and a half from my house,
a short distance by bike or on foot.
I never learned why they called it Parrot Street.
There were certainly no parrots in my town.
But there was the library:
large and square
built out of granite blocks
at the beginning of the last century.
A set of eight wide stone steps led to the front doors
with their thick beveled glass windows
that sent rainbows fluttering across the floor
when the sun shone through them.

And just beyond the doors
there was a polished, circular oak counter
where books were checked out and in.
The room on the left was for the grownups.
the one on the right for us children,
and presiding over them both
was the true blessing of my young life,
the librarian, Miss Elsie Groub.

Miss Groub was tall and thin.
Her bright red hair rested softly on her shoulders,
and what must have been a thousand freckles
danced across her narrow face.
She wore wire rimmed spectacles that always seemed
as if they were about to slip off the tip of her nose.
She loved two things in this world above all others,
books and children,
and her mission in life was to bring them together.
She would often recommend books for me to read.
When I returned them, I would tell Miss Groub
what I thought of them—sort of like an oral book report
only we never called it that.
I would speak. She would listen
and sometimes suggest another book I might like.

Once, when I was eight years old, she gave me a copy of
The Adventures of Tom Sawyer,
and what a book it was!
I felt as if I'd always known Tom and Becky and Huck and Aunt Polly.
I recognized where they lived and what they did.
And when I brought the book back to the library
I said, "Miss Groub, this is the best book I've ever read."

Just as if she had been waiting for me,
she pulled another book from under the counter
and handed it to me, saying,
"If you liked that one, you'll probably like this one also."
It was, of course, *The Adventures of Huckleberry Finn*.

Miss Groub was right.
She was righter than she could have ever guessed.
I did like it. I loved it – even more than Tom Sawyer.
I loved Huck and his friends and his howling wildness.
I yearned for his freedom and his adventures
along the Mississippi River.

I began reading it that very afternoon.
I read after supper, and when my mother and father went to bed,
which, in the time before television,
was much, much earlier than today.
I took my father's flashlight from his toolbox
and continued to read under the bed covers.
But no matter what the advertisements say
batteries wear out quickly, and it wasn't long
before the light went from bright to dim to none.

The book was so exciting that the next day
I skipped school for the very first time.
I went to the beach, sat on the rocks, and read.
I laughed. I was frightened. I cheered. I was sad.
I turned back to Huck Finn every moment I could.
I devoured the book the same way a lost and hungry dog
gobbles down the first food you give it.

A few days later I went running into the library, shouting,
"Miss Groub, Miss Groub, I was wrong.
Tom Sawyer isn't the best book in the world.
Huckleberry Finn is. It's the greatest book ever!"
And Miss Groub said something at that moment
that changed my life forever. She said,
"You know, the same man, Mark Twain,
wrote both those books."

I felt as if I had been struck by a lightning bolt.
I don't know what I thought up until that moment,
but for the first time I realized that human beings,
people just like you and me,
had written all those books that filled the shelves.
I must have been the dumbest kid in the world,
because, until then, the books were just there.
I made no connection between them
and anyone actually writing them.

But now, now everything was different,
and when the news sunk in, I said,
"Miss Groub, when I grow up, I'm going to be a writer,
and I'm going to write a better book than Huckleberry Finn."

That was more than fifty years ago.
I've been darkening pages with ink ever since.
I've published more than two dozen books.
I'm still trying to write a better book than
Mark Twain did with his Huckleberry Finn.
Whether I do or not
I'll not regret a single moment of trying,
and I owe it all to Miss Groub,
the librarian from the Parrot Street Public Library.

Postscript

A few years ago I found out that Miss Groub was living in a retirement home in Swampscott, Massachusetts. Early in the spring I went to visit her to thank her and to bring her some of my books. She was well into her 80s and her red hair had faded to a soft pink, but all those freckles still danced across her face and her spectacles still hung on the tip of her nose.

She told me she had known of my work since my first book. "I'm so happy and proud of you," she said. I thanked her for her inspiration and the guidance that led me to be a reader and a writer. We embraced and shared a few tears together.

I visited her again in the summer. We talked about books, past and present, and discovered that we shared many of the same favorites. She died that winter. Thank you, Miss Groub.

Steve Sanfield is poet, storyteller, children's author, and folklorist who resides on the San Juan Ridge

Library

MARILYN HARRIS KRIEGEL

WHAT do you do when you are 5'8", beginning Junior High School, and Marilyn Monroe and Jane Russell are the standards for beauty but you look like Twiggy, an ideal of attractiveness that will not occur to anyone for another 15 years? You try reading. You walk into the generally unused long rectangular library on the main floor of the run-down school in Elizabeth, New Jersey and you begin reading—anything. You start with the As and work your way around the room. You have three years to kill and this is as good a place as any to do your time.

One day a short guy with a salt-and-pepper crewcut pays attention to you. He's the librarian. When you're somewhere around the Ds he points out Dickens and mentions that if you ever want to backtrack you could check out Austen, Jane or Alcott, Louisa May. When you come in, he has nothing better to do than sit with his feet up on his battered desk and chat. He seems kind of stupid because he only wants to know what you think. He's really interested to know how swell you think George Eliot is, and though she was not one of his favorites, because of you he'll give her a second look. Her!

So this little guy can find a book to salve the most outrageous miseries, he can write passes to get you out of P. E., and he can encourage you to maybe write a book of your own—it seems that's something he has done himself once or twice and if you're interested he'll give you a copy of one of them—he'll even sign it—write a little note in the front about being your friend.

Since your parents think the business track in high school will do you just fine—accounting and typing, how to wrap packages for shipping, stuff like that—when the day arrives he can call his friend at the high school and get your program changed from vocational to academic. He can get you a spot on the High School paper. He can see that the play you write gets performed for Assembly. He can work magic in that public school library, making you believe in all sort of things, like that the world is pretty damn interesting and that writers like nothing better than to hang out with each other. He can believe in your mind. He can look up to you. His name is Gerald Raftery.

San Franciscan Marilyn Harris Kriegel was a Nevada County resident

The Key That Keeps On Turning

STEVE FJELDSTED

IN 1960 when I was barely six years old, our family moved to Anaheim, only a few miles from Disneyland. If my sister Linda and I had been behaving, we could stay up past 8 o'clock on summer nights to watch fireworks from our front porch. We only lived there about a year, but the time seems so memorable, probably because of the fundamental milestones reached there. I first learned to read on my cowboy bedspread, to ride a bike on our crooked driveway, and received my first library card only a few blocks away. The first book I checked out was *Curious George*, about a little primate with whom I could identify.

We moved several more times during my childhood, often enough that I couldn't have a dog, or at least that's what I was told. But no matter what, my library card helped provide companionship. Now I realize that it was my key to the real Magic Kingdom, the wonderful world of books. Soon I was tearing through Dr. Seuss and the Hardy Boys. Then it was on to L. Frank Baum and Sherlock Holmes. As life changing as these reading experiences were, it wasn't for 20 years that I ever thought about becoming a librarian.

Not long before enrolling for Library School at San Jose State in 1979, I wasn't so sure what I wanted to do for a living. At times I'd wanted to be a sportswriter, a poet, a teacher, or an athlete. But my world completely rotated when I first encountered Myrt, the Branch Librarian for the Turlock Library. I was living in an 80-year-old house, surrounded by fruit trees, while attending English classes and playing on the basketball team at Stanislaus State.

I have indelible recollections of the enthusiasm Myrt exuded. She obviously loved helping people and took great joy in the spirit of discovery. It was almost as though she was an usherette at the Pearly Gates who was handing out as many free passes as possible. She even let me photocopy my turgid poetry on the library's machine. Her attitude contrasted sharply to that of some of the librarians at the college who wanted to deny me the use of some Coleridge titles in the locked case, even though I had the required student library card.

From my usual spot at a study table, Myrt was unwaveringly friendly and professional in her many dealings with the public. It seemed like she was acquainted with practically everyone in town and almost every book on the shelves. She also served as a positive role model for me at a time when I really needed one, although I didn't know it back then. Clearly, Myrt has exerted a greater impact on my life than all my heroes combined. She's like Steinbeck, Mother Theresa, John Wooden, and Jimmy Stewart all rolled into one. Only more.

A couple of years later I received my English degree, and started working as a circulation clerk at the Modesto Library. Unexpectedly, Myrt walked in and I awkwardly tried to express my admiration. My approach was undoubtedly clumsy and she understandably kept going, adding that the air was getting pretty thick. I felt like I'd blown my only chance to express my admiration. Within a few months I left to pursue librarianship at San Jose State and lost track of her, although memories returned regularly. Usually I thought of her when I was helping someone at one of the libraries where I worked, including the same Anaheim Library where my odyssey began.

Since then I've worked at many other libraries, mostly in the San Joaquin Valley. But it wasn't until about three years ago, after I'd begun as the Nevada County Librarian, that a local resident named Rob and his daughter visited the Madelyn Helling Library and relayed the message from his aunt, "Myrt says hello." Instantly, I knew to whom he was referring. After getting her address I wrote a letter to finally inform her of my long-held esteem. I wasn't so sure she'd even remember me, but she replied with a wonderful letter, informing me that her staff used to secretly call me "Steve with a J," a nickname I'd never heard.

By now I've worked almost 30 years in libraries, and I've known a lot of truly remarkable and unforgettable people, but if it wasn't for Myrt, I probably wouldn't have met any of them.

Steve Fjeldsted, the former Nevada County Librarian, bats left and can almost throw right; he was traded to Southern California for two Buffalo Springfield albums, a Kirk Gibson autograph, and a future draft pick

A Utopian Democracy

DENNIS CARR

"CHECK the overcoat pockets in the closet." I could tell by Mom's anxious voice that we needed to find some change for the bus fare or things were going to get ugly. I had already checked the overcoats and was now turning over the sofa cushions, but without success. Suddenly I thought of emptying the bottles of Pepsi from the icebox into the roasting pan to turn in the bottles for the deposit. All this effort to get round-trip bus fare for my mom so we could head to the Richmond Hill Public Library to satisfy her insatiable desire for another week's worth of murder mysteries. The bottle deposits netted 24 cents, and with the two cents from my sister's penny loafers, we were on our way. I, as usual, would have to sneak past the bus driver to avoid paying the fare. At the age of nine, I was four years beyond free passage, something Mom hated to accept.

"Hey lady, what about the kid?" the driver yelled for all to hear as I quickly scrambled to the back, using a lady with large shopping bags to shield my presence.

"He's still five," Mom replied loudly.

"Yeah, on what leg, lady?"

The driver was clearly not convinced.

In a voice that could not be ignored, she replied, "Oh, why don't you stop picking on a poor lady with four kids, and just drive your damn bus."

That did it! Not only did the driver clam up, but so did every passenger on the bus as we rolled down Lefferts Boulevard en route to the peace and comfort of the Richmond Hill Library.

It was a beautiful and inviting library, an old Carnegie. The building oozed welcome and character as well as style. The smell of books massed in a library produces a tranquilizing effect on me. I could enter a library stressed and tense and leave a half hour later at peace with the world. It wasn't the nearest library to our house; in fact, there were at least three others that we could have walked to. But, living in New York, with over 100 libraries citywide, even poor folks like us had choices, and Mom was one who liked to choose.

The stacks were filled with new releases, all the classics and a rich section of non-fiction. It also contained the main reason for our venture, a very large section of murder mysteries. Mom was addicted to books; she had a five-to-seven-book-a-week habit, and, being poor, the only way to feed her habit was through the New York Public Library system.

Mrs. Applebaum, the librarian, immediately waved to us, giving Mom a muted greeting and me a big hug, maintaining the required silence. It took no time for Mom and Mrs. Applebaum to become close buddies once Mrs. A. learned Mom was a murder mystery devotee like herself. "Mary, I have some juicy murders for you hidden away in the back." Mom beamed with pleasure as I headed to the history section for any book on Davy Crockett.

I noticed very early on that wealth did not matter here. Rich or poor, all had equal standing. Long before the civil rights movement began, libraries practiced unbiased access. All one needed was a library card and the self-restraint to speak quietly. The public library is a fine example of perfect democracy and Mrs. A. was the guardian of Utopia. She was like an over-indulgent parent. She could not do enough for us once she knew we were addicted to her treasures. The ability to walk into a public establishment without a cent and be treated so well was almost too good to be true. Free public libraries are without doubt a wonderful resource. While checking out our books, Mrs. A. would hold a finger to her lips and slip us a bag of homemade macaroons, my favorite!

Happily toting five pounds of murder mysteries, Mom and I headed to the bus stop for the trip home. This time the bus strategy was modified. While Mom entered the front door, paying her fare and distracting the driver, I slipped onto the bus from the rear exit, shielded by exiting passengers. It worked like a charm! Amidst hostile stares from our fellow travelers, we read our books and ate macaroons, ever grateful to Mr. Carnegie and Mrs. Applebaum.

Dennis Carr lives in Penn Valley

Miss Whatever

BY CHRIS CASEY

THAT winter was particularly cold and dark ... and long ... and sad. My dad came into town from the farm every Wednesday. Mom always seemed to be at a church meeting and so I would just sit with Dad and listen; listen to his childhood memories, listen to his regrets, listen to his sadness.

I don't really remember why Dad and I decided to go to the library that Wednesday evening in January. Maybe I had an overdue book, or maybe I had a book review for school, or maybe my dad and I were just tired of being alone together. I do remember the snow.

The town library was once home to a well-to-do family. However, this Midwest town no longer had any well-to-do families; they had all moved on or died off. Fortunately for the town, this family left their home to the community for use as the public library before passing through to other lives. Consequently, four days a week those of us left behind could experience the splendor of high-ceilinged rooms, parquet flooring, and pillared archways, as we searched the bookshelves for "take-out dreams."

As my dad and I trudged up the stone steps to the wide covered porch I proudly pointed out the hours, rules, and layout of the library itself as a frequent visiting expert. Upon entering the overheated interior, however, my voice became a whisper as I looked to the right to see THE LIBRARIAN. She sat sternly behind the large and cluttered mahogany desk that served as office, public counter, circulation desk, reference library, and cataloguing department. I don't remember her name, although it definitely started with MISS and she was right out of central casting for the typical librarian or spinster aunt in any Hollywood production of an old English classic.

I mumbled "hi," without really making eye contact, as I made a beeline for the anteroom that served as the children's library. Miss Whatever's reply assured me that she was no more pleased to see me, even if Dad and I were the only other living creatures sharing her evening in this overly warm and quiet island in the snow. My ears told me, however, that Dad had stopped at the desk/office to further introduce himself and discuss the details of the winter weather outside.

I quickly located the few mystery books left on the shelves that I hadn't already read at least once. I'd long ago checked out every dog and horse book available and was NOT at all interested in the sappy pre-teen romances sitting on the top shelves reserved for "Junior High Patrons Only." As I returned to the desk/checkout counter, however, I saw my dad and Miss Whatever engrossed in conversation. To my dismay, this almost animated discussion showed no signs of abating as I alternately stood, sat, paced, and sighed the time away. We left at nine, an hour past closing!

And so our Wednesday evenings were redefined by these literary visitations. After an early dinner and Mom leaving for another church meeting, Dad and I drove through the snow (always snowing) to the "mansion" where my dad selected a few historical biographies ("much more interesting than fiction") and renewed his conversation with Miss Whatever. We never had to worry about "competing" for the librarian's attention, as other patrons were scarce to the point of non-existence.

Gradually, I also settled into the rhythm of these visits and eventually became aware of the advantages to be gleaned from this strange friendship between my dad and the old woman behind the desk. Unnoticed, I began to peruse the adult bookshelves, thumbing through the classics and a few of the more innocent best-sellers. Finding my dad, as he visited the two feet of shelves marked "Biography," I would whisper my request that he check out my selection of "banned to children" books.

Some evenings I even sat and listened as my dad and Miss Whatever discussed the advantages of country living, the lack of intellectualism in today's youth, and the general decline of civilization since the advent of television. At one point, Dad exposed our little deception—that, in fact, I was the one that would be reading the Agatha Christie mystery, as he assured her I was intellectually mature enough to handle Miss Marple's adventures. To my surprise, Miss Whatever almost smiled and agreed.

And so it went. Eventually it stopped snowing, the drifts melted, and my dad's visits were less predictable. When I did see him we planted in the garden or played catch. My visits to the library continued, solo, on Saturday mornings. One morning Miss Whatever asked how "Gordon" was doing and I said "OK." She continued to let me check out books from the adult section, but asked that I only do it when no one else was around. She and I even chatted at times and I told the other kids she really "wasn't that bad."

One day a year or so later another librarian greeted me on my weekly visit. She was very big and looked more like a school principal or a pastor's wife than a librarian. I never saw Miss Whatever again, which was odd, as it was difficult not to see someone living in a little town of two thousand (in a good year when nobody froze to death). Once in a while Dad would ask about Miss Whatever. "There's a story to everyone," he would tell me with a shadow of a smile.

Chris Casey lives in Nevada City

In the Library. *Pencil drawing by Rachel Unruh, age 7*

The Best of Times

GLENNIS M. DOLE

ALTHOUGH there is evidence of Saxon and Roman presence in the general area, the small town of Nelson, in the industrial NW region of England, is a typical Lancashire mill town. Its development was based on the textile industry—first wool then cotton, which was transported to town by canal from the port of Liverpool. The first free public library in Nelson was established in 1889 in rooms over the market hall in the centre of town. In 1895 it was transferred to the Technical School, located just a few streets away. The town received a Carnegie Grant of £7,000 and a new library was built and opened in 1908. It was a big Edwardian building, next door to the central fire station, and across the street from a Wesleyan Chapel.

It was a typical building of its era—steps at the front, imposing entrance, mosaic tiles in the central hallway. It looked like a library ought to look. The main floor housed the general section. The reference department was upstairs and the children's library in the basement.

Like most children of my generation, I started school at age four and a half and could read very well a year later. This was the early 1940s—books were precious and scarce and we were not allowed to take school books home. That was the bad part. The good part was that one could join the library at age seven. My mother had to take me for the initial obligatory filling out of the application card, but after that I was allowed to go alone. It seems trite to describe my library experience as a love affair, but it was. And still is.

As usual in stories like this, there is a heroine, and in this tale, as in so many, it is the children's librarian. For many years I called her "Miss." I didn't know her name and wouldn't have presumed to use it if I had. Because of the war, most of our teachers were women and we called them all "Miss." The library Miss was a stern but fair person who instilled, through a sort of osmosis, not only a love of books but a respect for them. My feelings about books are the same today as they were all those years ago.

The rules were few, but quite rigid. The borrowing period was two weeks. One had two library cards, one for fiction and one for non-fiction. The fiction card could be used for a non-fiction book, but not vice versa. This was useful in later years, for homework and the like, but frustrating if one had a favourite fiction author and there were two books available at the same time. In special circumstances, such as illness, Miss could be persuaded by a parent to issue an extra fiction card or two for a limited period of time. Such cards had the heading "Temporary Ticket" in red ink and were signed and dated. I never had a temporary card but I did see one once, and learned that Miss' name was E. Holden.

Sometimes when I visited the library there would be a group of older children who seemed to be more than just library patrons. Not only did they stand around behind the desk and generally help out, but they were allowed to talk and had that air of knowing secrets. I envied them because they seemed to know things, and because E. Holden had real conversations with them. I didn't know why, but I desperately wanted to be one of them.

We all changed schools in our early teens, and at my new school I became friendly with a girl who was a member of that wonderful clique. I learned from her that it had a name—the Library Guild—and that the members were hand-picked. The only way in was to be introduced by a current member and then write a formal letter of application. My friend made the introduction, I was vetted, quietly encouraged to apply, and accepted. I learned how to check books in and out, to guide new young borrowers, to shelve, to count the end-of-day transactions, to use the card catalogue and—best of all—how to prepare new books for general circulation.

I loved this job because it meant actually handling new books. It was a real glimpse into the backstairs world of the library and it involved lots of rubber stamping. The most magnificent stamp was reserved for the top of the first page of text. It read:

> PLEASE DO NOT MARK, SOIL, GET WET,
> OR TURN DOWN THE LEAVES OF THIS BOOK.

Just typing that takes me right back to that special time and place, and to the memory of that amazing lady. She encouraged us to see beyond our humble backgrounds and look towards a bigger world. From her we learned how to discuss without arguing, to make the most of our educational opportunities, and to help younger people come to love books and reading as we did. She was our mentor before the word became fashionable or overused and we all knew we were special. She had other interests but I think the Library Guild was always her greatest passion.

Glennis M. Dole lives in Grass Valley

Keepers of the Culture

DALE JACOBSON

"THE *liberry is for macking you grow up more smurter if you can do it and gittin lots of riting and reeding."* This perhaps less-than-erudite author could have been me. On many an afternoon, when I escaped from Nevada City Elementary School, I would scurry one and a fifth blocks down to a large square grey building that looked like a small penitentiary for Confederate soldiers. I would open the heavy outside door and run up the cold stone stairs to the big warm room. The smell of old musty literature would engulf me like a fog as I made my way to the medieval front desk, and "My People."

Ancient, large, quiet women ran the joint, whom I presume left the frantic pace of the convent for the tranquility and control of silent monolithic rows of knowledge and wisdom. These sturdy, ample women would sit me on their ample laps and make me read aloud to them. These silent sentinels guarding the culture taught me to sort out jumbled alphabet letters until I could create actual words, and re-create them. Then came sentences, then paragraphs, then full pages, then full books, so that I could one day read poetry. Thus, I was thankful and proud to oblige them, and read on their nourishing laps at great length. Promptly, after the "Dick, Jane, and Spot the Dog" stories ran out of subject content, I branched out into even bigger books with bigger words with bigger plots.

My first bigger book to read, mostly on my own, was called *A Yankee Flyer in the R.A.F.* It was about the handsome Stanley, an American Air Force pilot who, after his amazing adventures, could hold a whole quarter of a pie in his hand and eat it. If you don't believe me go read the book! (It was a green hardbound toward the middle on the top right shelf of the children's section to the left of the set of Hardy Boys books.)

Luckily, the book was part of a four-book series, so I was able to read about the brave and good American Stanley, and the almost-as-good English pilots, courageously dog-fighting the very bad German Nazi pilots. The well-intentioned but silently scowling librarians were not happy with my choosing war books, but what do such innocent women know of such glorious escapades? How could women see the Nazi Luftwaffe coming while standing at the stove and kitchen sink wiping noses? Such knowledge and appreciation of glory is reserved for us "manly men."

My Christmas wish that year—after saving all the little children of the world—was a big model army set. Just kidding .... about the children, that is! Many an afternoon and evening I would spend in deep silence at the long tables covered with magazines and newspapers, reading any and all subjects. Where else could you learn that the Christian Doukhobors (meaning "spirit wrestlers") originated in Russia, immigrated to Canada, and were a religious sect who believed that churches, government, and clothing were of the devil, and thus felt abandoned by God during their first Canadian winter though they were stark naked? I searched out the encyclopedias and old *Life* and *National Geographic* magazines for writing school reports, while learning to be quiet and respectful.

Now, years later, the ingredients of the quiet old "Confederate prison," along with the noisy old county jail, have been moved to bigger, fancier buildings, complete with computers and security systems. Due to new legal-beagle ramifications ... no sitting on laps and no Shhhhshs for young 'uns! (Anti-depressant drug company studies might indicate that "shushhhhing" a child creates feelings of abandonment and lack of self-esteem, thus necessitating Ritalin!) The newly-passed Patriot Act tells the librarians to report back to Big Brother on who reads what books, and who watches what videos, and when the deeds were done.

My kids—and OK, me too!—now have fancy computers with Internet access, which possess absolutely no warm laps, no quaint odors of antiquity, no long dark neatly ordered tables, and no crashing echoes of pins dropped at the far end of halls. Perhaps my children could have become, like many, most unfortunately oblivious to the wise counsel and spiritual nourishment flowing in abundance from the traditional laps of the gracious old wise women. But, then, God graciously intervened with a significantly less silent sentinel, and I married their mama.

Dale Jacobson, chiropractor, lives in Nevada City

How to Catch a Match

MARY ANN TRYGG

IT worked for me. It could for you too. In many years of service to the public in libraries of all sizes, I had heard about it, even seen it for myself in one specific instance. But that was typical—employees working together day after day. Single employees. It's heaven for the men. Shall we say 20 to one? Women versus men. In this profession, particularly in public libraries, the librarians are the born teacher-types, who really care about others and want to help with research, and instruct them on how to find what they're seeking. Librarians open the doors each day to all who seek their own kind of comfort, knowledge, recreation, and/or personal enrichment. The Library is a community gathering place where all are looked upon not exactly equally, but more equally than in most other places that come to mind.

"It was a dark and stormy night...." Truly, it was, in the autumn of 1992. I was working at the Grass Valley Library as the Children's Librarian, when who should walk in out of the rain but THE ONE—my future husband. He looked vaguely familiar. The library wasn't busy, but my co-worker Joan and I were providing our own particular brand of attentive library service until closing time at eight p.m. It was pouring outside. Our library patrons always took center stage when they arrived, especially on an evening like this. We visited. My, this was a chatty one!

And then I found out. We had a lot in common. I had just completed my divorce; he was in the middle of his. Our children knew each other before we did. They went to the same school. That's where I'd seen him. Band performances. He was a dedicated parent. So was I. Never missed an open house or parent conference. His soon-to-be ex-wife said later that it made perfect sense. Meeting a woman in a library! He had taken *her* to the Cal State Fullerton Library on their first date way back when. He took to coming around. Reading the papers, checking out the business books. This ulterior motive is so easy at the library.

What I'm trying to say is that romance in the library is a natural. I'm sorry, but we can't all be librarians in this world. The profession is a noble one and tremendously rewarding, but even if you aren't a librarian, which means, by the way, that you have actually gone to college, obtained a Bachelor's and then a Master's Degree in Library Science, it could still happen to you the other way. Remember how you told your parents you were going to the library to study when you obtained the all-important driver's license and borrowed a set of wheels from your parents?

Well, from that first inclination to fabricate the truth a little, you were headed in the right direction. I have to admit that I actually did go to the library at that tender age. But for all of you who may not have heard, it is the place to meet someone special. Guaranteed. The proof came later for me, but library degree or no, hang out in a library, even in several libraries for maximum opportunities and you may just find that while flipping through the DVDs, videos, music CDs, or lost in the stacks, a special someone may start up the conversation that leads to true love. I had 40 hours a week to devote and it only took one year for me. For others, being unemployed can be a bonus.

Oh yes, I've read about the love generated in libraries. Truth is, I read about other libraries more than the average person on the street, and what Eric and I contemplated wasn't unheard of. Lots of couples (well perhaps not "lots") have gotten married in their local library. Maybe not a library that has a life-sized cutout of a gold lame-clad Elvis, but the place of that first meeting is the key. Just another public service.

We envisioned the dogs coming too because, you see, we were active in Guide Dogs for the Blind at the time. My daughter had recently graduated her dog, Delsie, and the club members wanted to be part of the wedding. And of course, none of us really went very many places without the dogs coming too. I could tell you about one of our first dates. Something to do with pooper scooping, but I'll hold off on that one for another time. In the end, we married in our church, but I sometimes think of the way it might have been to walk up the stairs of the old Carnegie Grass Valley Library to say "I do."

My point—librarian or not, you too can find your life mate at the library. Hey, we've got all the books you'll ever need on interpersonal relationships, engagement and wedding planning, so you can study up while waiting. It's free and it's a big step up from people-watching in front of Flour Garden bakery on a warm spring morning (which I also recommend), and everyone is welcome. It worked for me. It could for you too.

Mary Ann Trygg is the Nevada County Librarian

Right There in the Stacks
ROBERT LOBELL

I love my library, and I love my librarian. And I'm not the only one. I
 know a lot of guys like
me who can't help sneakin' peeks at them through the bookshelves,
 and even fantasize about
making love right there in the stacks surrounded by romance novels,
 risking discovery by jealous
patrons. Seems like some guys prefer to check out the librarians
 instead of the books.
But what's the attraction? No offense, but we're usually not talking
 Playboy Bunnies here,
rather the prim and proper type, with closed collars, heavy-framed
 eyeglasses strung from their
necks, no leg showing, and graying hair pinned up in a severely tamed
 bun. No, the attraction is
something more intangible, like maturity combined with competence,
 intelligence, and the kind
of no-nonsense personality men just love submitting to. There's just
 something about those
spiritual qualities that turn on middle-aged guys like myself.
Yes, I love my library, but I love my librarian even more, especially
 when she said yes to my
marriage proposal in the back of the poetry aisle. I just wish Dewey
 Decimal could've been best man at the wedding.

Robert Lobell lives in Nevada City

Two Kisses

MALCOLM MARGOLIN

I WAS born in Boston, in the urban and gritty neighborhood of Dorchester, at an urban and gritty time, 1940. The first library I remember was an intimate neighborhood library with two rooms, one for adults, the other for children. A children's librarian held sway, enforced the code of silence, assessed fines of one or two cents for overdue books, and sagely nodded approval at my selections. I don't remember that my choices were especially literary. All I can recall now are endless variations of the same adventure story—unexplored planets, undiscovered continents, secret valleys, hidden attics, lost treasures, unsolved crimes, all manner of wealth guarded by hostile forces that were variously Indians, pirates, outlaws, and their generally swarthy, stonehearted brethren. The reading level, I suspect, was that of comic books, but without pictures. But they were books, entertaining and offering vicarious outdoor adventures and romantic escape in a world that provided far too little of the real thing. As an added bonus, in the Jewish household in which I grew up books—any and all books, whatever the subject—were sacred and worthy. "Malcolm's reading a book. Don't disturb him." When you are eight or nine, you take what little power and prestige you can get, and I took it with gratitude.

When I got to high school, a different experience was in store. I could now walk from Boston Public Latin School near the downtown area to the main Boston Public Library in Copley Square. I remember approaching the grand staircase guarded by stone lions, the wondrously huge doors that opened and closed with incomprehensible fullness and ease. I remember galleries of paintings and an inner courtyard with sculptures; large curving marble stairs that led to the second floor; a cavernous reading room with long wooden tables, its pervasive late afternoon gloom punctuated by the warm light of Tiffany lamps; the frieze upon which was carved the names of great thinkers and scholars; and lining the walls of the main reading room shelves not so much of books but of tomes weighted with wisdom and authority. I remember placing my book bag on a wooden table, flicking on a lamp, and heading for the reference desk. A dignified man with a suit and tie, or a woman formally attired in a dark dress and white blouse, would be there to answer questions or offer guidance, treating my inquiries about some dopey homework assignment with gravity, thoughtfulness, and concern before withdrawing into the recesses to retrieve just the right book. I couldn't have been better treated if I had been a Nobel Laureate.

I have a confession to make. I did not come to the library just to study, but to meet a girl. Her name was Ruth. We were both shy, and the furthest I ever got was "footsie" under the table, and once on the way out she pressed her breasts against me and we kissed a kiss so fragrant and full that fifty years later I still remember it. Adolescent urges drove me to that great edifice of learning. But the Boston Public Library, opulent and well appointed, had nevertheless an immense effect, one that lingered long after Ruth and I went separate ways, an effect that certainly helped shape my life. All that elegance and grandeur carried an important, heady message to a confused teenager from Dorchester. The message, simply put, was this: that the society at large, the public civic culture, a culture supported by taxing immigrants and laborers and shopkeepers, so valued books and learning that it would provide not just minimal and begrudging services but marble staircases, men in suits, and Tiffany lamps to those who would pursue the pathways of knowledge. Reading was valued, encouraged, and rewarded with a lavish building and aristocratic service.

Surely this perception that reading and books were of such unassailable value contributed to my choosing a literary life. And, as a publisher and writer, that is indeed the life I have lived for some forty years now. While in financial terms it's meant (despite my best efforts) an involuntary vow of lifelong poverty, I've never felt in the least bit poor. Rather, I've always felt well taken care of, valued, treated by the world with great tenderness, generosity, and even opulence. Some of that feeling, I'm sure, is drawn from those wonderful memories of the Boston Public Library.

Malcolm Margolin, Berkeley, is the Publisher of
Heyday Books and News From Native California

Not Studying

MOLLY FISK

I WENT to a fancy college back East and one of my many peculiar jobs was to water the plants in Radcliffe's Hilles Library. Every week I took a huge watering can out of the maintenance closet, filled it with water from a big slate sink that smelled of disinfectant, and lugged it from floor to floor, refilling three times as I went.

The library was a four-story glass affair built in the early '70s, and most of the plants I watered were on the middle landings of the staircases, between the floors. On Thursday nights you could stand outside and watch me do the whole routine—I know this because it's how my boyfriend got up his nerve to introduce himself. The plants were ficus trees, of course, those tropical imports that someone decided should grace every public building in America. They're beautiful and lacy, and when placed beside plate glass walls on the south side of a library, need to be watered more than once a week.

I knew nothing about plants at this time and couldn't figure out whether the yellow leaves that dropped from these two south-side trees were a sign of too much water or too little. I was nervous that I was killing them, but my boss was a gruff maintenance supervisor who was hard to find. I didn't know who else to ask and didn't want to admit to failure.

As I was weighing my options, dreading the autumnal pile of leaves I would find under these trees, they began to recover. Each week I picked up fewer dead leaves and the ones still on the branches looked happier. It was very mysterious, until the night I went with my boyfriend to study for a final and met one of the librarians with a watering can on the stairs. She smiled, a little guiltily. I smiled back, gratefully. There's more than one way a librarian can save you.

Hilles Library was a fine place to go with your boyfriend if you were really going to study. Those glass walls made it hard to do anything else. If you had other things in mind, you went to Widener, the enormous main college library, and snuck into the stacks. My major was Folklore & Mythology, an excellent choice because that section was to be found on Level C, three floors underground. No one was ever down there. I spent some of my happiest college hours on the musty carpet of level C, engaged in an ancient and popular practice—although of course we thought we'd invented it—sandwiched between Mircea Eliade's *The Sacred and the Profane* and the Fitzgerald translation of Homer's *Iliad*.

Molly Fisk is a poet and essayist in Nevada City

Heartfelt Expression

BARBARA JONES

My Dearest Love,

While we have known each other for years, it is only within the last several that I have begun to truly know you. I am honored by your request regarding my perception of our relationship (i.e. what you mean to me) for it shows you care about me too. I am afraid there are not enough words in even the biggest Webster's dictionary to express my love for you.

You are like a cool breeze in the summer and like a warm, welcoming hug in the winter. You are so willing to share your quiet, peaceful home that you attract many interesting people of all ages. Like me, they respect you and value your vast array of knowledge.

You have provided me with hours and hours of entertainment Your stories have made me laugh and cry. I have shared many of your stories with other friends. I feel like I have traveled around the world and met people in many exotic lands through your stories. You have shared information about Feng Shui, parenting, gardening, art, geography, spirituality and multiple other subjects so that I feel I have learned more from you than all my years in public school

I know there are others like you around the world. Maybe they are really stacked and robust but you are mine. You have always been there for me and have allowed me to stroke your spines longingly for hours. You have forgiven even my greatest indiscretion of leaving a book in the rain. And when I get too far away and haven't visited you in a while, you always send me a little note reminding me that you miss me.

You are my best friend, my teacher, my true love.

Barbara Jones lives in Nevada City

How Do I Love the Library? Let Me Count the Ways

PAM JUNG

I LOVE rewarding myself at the end of an intense workday by a trip to the library, where I can browse, pretending I am a lady of leisure. I love the delicious moment when I sit down in an easy chair with a magazine in hand, knowing that for the next half hour I have nowhere else to go and nothing else to do.

I love the smell of the library.

I love being with other readers, who though lost in their own worlds of newspaper, book, magazine are like co-conspirators in this quest for knowledge, or maybe just for information (there is a difference, you know), or perhaps we're all simply escaping into a world of imagination.

Whatever, I love the company.

I love the magic of being transported to other worlds, the unlimitedness of the possibilities, as I leaf through a book I'm considering. Will I travel to the Congo? Will I overhear a supposed conversation between the Viennese physician Dr. Breuer and the tormented philosopher Friederich Nietzsche? Or will I feel the terror of what it's like to find myself alone in outer space?

I love knowing that if I somehow falter in my search for whatever it is I'm searching for, a serviceful librarian will be there to help me figure it out. I love having choices that are based on how I'm feeling. Yes to that book. No to that one. How lovely, being in touch with my mood of the moment. I love the quiet of the library. Fie on that whiney child or those chatty teens. I'm told it's old-fashioned to whisper like days of old, yet that's exactly what I do, just as if I were in a monastery.

I love the excited feeling I get when I bring my booty home and pop the cassette or CD of a book on tape into my player, wondering will I like the sound of the narrator's voice? Will the reader capture the correct cadence of the story? Listening to books is trippy. It beats reading when eyes feel like hard boiled eggs after eight hours on a computer.

I love the library because it is so good to me.

Pam Jung, Nevada City, is the Editor of The Prospector, *The Union's Arts and Entertainment section*

A Brief Reverie
SUZANNE KOLICHE

He's not so much sick as he is sickly
   and that's why I visit him regularly.
I check his medications, pulse and lungs.
Periodically we go off track and chat,
   while I methodically enter data in the lap-top.

One day he tells me how very much he misses reading. We sit with this, silently. After a pause I say "How about audio tapes from the library."

"The library," he says with true awe in his voice.
"When I was a kid, we went once a week and I had the choice of three books. Yep. I always got one book on building, one mystery book—you know, detective type—
   there was a series that I really liked—and a book about people, a biography."

We are sitting in the sturdy, manly, earthy house that he constructed. "I guess you really studied those how-to-build-it books" I gesture towards the kitchen with its finely crafted hutch and then swoop my hand around to encompass the whole. "Look at what you've built!"

He's smiling big now. He loves his home and well he should.
Stone foundation laid in the eager boy's mind so long ago.
Hand-made furnishings. A nice floor plan.
Large arched windows. French doors with dark polished wood.
He nods. "Yep. Going to the library shaped my way, from idea to goal,
   from child to man, from rough-hewn to carved, curved and smoothed."

We sit in the pleasant woodsy quiet of the house he built.

We sit in the quiet, each
   drifting in a brief reverie,
   each remembering a beloved childhood library.

Suzanne Koliche lives in Nevada City

A Place to Dream the Impossible

ARIANNE WING

ONE of my earliest recollections of going to a library is being mesmerized by the *ka-chunk* the date-stamp made when the librarian checked out books. I was about three-and-a-half years old when my mother began taking my siblings and me on weekly trips to the library. The Hanford Library was then located in a *grande dame* of a building, built by funds donated by Andrew Carnegie. I remember holding my mother's hands as we walked up the steps and her lifting me up to drink from the porcelain drinking fountain. That ritual complete, we entered the small area sectioned off for children's books. Books were stacked on a table and on the window sills, as well as on the shelves. I can still summon up the scents of lemon oil and books old and new.

I loved the book *Bedtime for Frances*, and borrowed it from the library again and again. When the librarian retired the book, she gave it to me, knowing how much I loved it. I brought the book home and welcomed it with grape juice spilled from my Fred Flintstone jelly glass. Then it was officially my book.

My father loved to tell us stories at bedtime. He might start to read from a book but then he'd put the book down and tell us a tale on his own, usually some adventure of King Arthur and the Knights of the Round Table. During the next visit to the library I would look for more stories about the people of Camelot and The Holy Grail. No wonder libraries still have for me the quality of the numinous.

I fell in love with many authors; I'm still doing that today. As a child I wrote a fan letter to Beverly Cleary and was thrilled beyond thrilled to receive her reply. I took her letter to school for Show and Tell.

The Library outgrew itself and a new one was built, the one I frequent today. The little library is now a museum, and these days I have a library of my own. While I do go to my local library for readings and events, I less frequently check out book than when I was a child. The sense of quiet, sacred space I learned as a child, however, is still with me. The library is the place to seek answers and the sacred.

Originally in front of the new Hanford Library was a sculpture of Don Quixote, a signal that a library is a place to dream the impossible dream. Indeed, where else?

It is also the place of stillness that somehow quickens, a place of family memories, a place that was both an inspiration and key to my own quest to become one day a writer. Why not? Impossible dreams can come true. Especially when one has that certain piece of The Holy Grail in her hand, a library card.

Arianne Wing of Hanford is the author of Rays of Hope

Good Friday World

ANNE LAMOTT

I AM going to walk to the library, because my church is too far away to go to on foot. And it's so beautiful out. The hills of my town are lush and green and dotted with wildflowers. The poppies have bloomed, and as summer approaches, five o'clock is no longer the end of the world. I am going to check out a collection of *Goon Show* scripts, and a volume of Mary Oliver poems. Libraries make me think kindly of my mother. I am not sure if this will lead me directly to the soupçon of forgiveness, but you never know. You take the action, and the insight follows. It was my mother who taught me how to wander through the racks of the Belvedere-Tiburon Library, and wander through a book, letting it take me where it would. She and my father took me to the library every week when I was little. One of her best friends was the librarian. They both taught me that if you insist on having a destination when you come into a library, you're shortchanging yourself. They read to live, the way they also went to the beach, or ate delicious food. Reading was like breathing fresh ocean air, or eating tomatoes from old man Grbac's garden. My parents, and librarians along the way, taught me about the space between words; about the margins, where so many juicy moments of life and spirit and friendship could be found. In a library, you can find small miracles and truth, and you might find something that will make you laugh so hard that you will get shushed, in the friendliest way. I have found sanctuary in libraries my whole life, and there is sanctuary there now, from the war, from the storms of our families and our own minds. Libraries are like mountains or meadows or creeks: sacred space. So this afternoon, I'll walk to the library.

Anne Lamott's latest book is Grace (Eventually): Thoughts on Faith; *she lives in Fairfax, and this excerpt is from "Good Friday World,"* Plan B: Further Thoughts on Faith

Ethiopia

UTAH PHILLIPS

IT'S along about 1944—I guess I was nine years old at the time. I was living in the old Jewish ghetto in Cleveland, Ohio. My mother had remarried Sid Cohen, a young Jewish businessman, and he moved us into his father's neighborhood (my grandfather, Simon Bialabjetski), a loud boisterous neighborhood. They still had horses in the streets—they never gave them up because of gas rationing—but it was a neighborhood that was becoming more and more circumscribed as a black population moved in on one edge and an Italian population moved in on the other edge. Consequently, the neighborhood became more dangerous, especially for kids, and we had gangs. I was in the Orville St. Gutter Rats.

It was easy to get beat up coming home from school. I went to Doan School, which was only a block and a half from my house—we lived on Orville St. I didn't like getting pounded on on my way home from school. So I would wait in school after everybody had left, as long as I could, say till about four in the afternoon, when the janitor finally threw me out. And then I would run straight across 105th to the little library, the little community library across the street. Sometimes with kids on my heels. And I'd race through the door and the librarian would be right there and say, "You can't do that here!" and she'd keep those kids out. And then I'd stay there till about five or so, until I felt safe to go home.

While I was there, the librarian gave me books, and one of the first books she gave me was a kid's book about Ethiopia. My situation was pretty tenuous, you know; my father had disappeared, nobody told me what happened, I was in a neighborhood that spoke Yiddish—a foreign language to me—and here I was in this school I didn't understand. Getting my mind as far away from that reality as it would go was a good idea, and Ethiopia was it. I still have a whole shelf of books about Ethiopia which I study any time I want to relax.

Well, that's what the library means to me. First of all, it engendered a love of books. But most of all, as I've traveled for the past 36 years in my trade, sometimes doing a lot of political work, picket-line work and so on, whenever I felt threatened, whenever I felt really alienated, whenever I felt lonely, whatever town I was in, I'd head for the public library and sit there and feel perfectly safe. That's why I have a library in my home: The Brownell Library of Popular Antiquities. I feel perfectly safe when I sit in the library in my house. If I'm putting together shows to go on the road, if I have to do some writing, you can count on finding me at the Madelyn Helling Library, sitting at one of the big round tables where I do my best work, because I feel perfectly comfortable and perfectly safe.

And that's my story.

Utah Phillips, Nevada City, is a traveling folksinger, storyteller, and provocateur

Josiah Royce Library, Grass Valley. *Drawing by Joan Brown*

Dogs

LUCINDA SAHM DELORIMIER

HERE'S the deal: Not only are they open to all, libraries, but once you're in there, everything is open to all. My sister has been getting these little terriers from Ireland, little tough-guy people, black and tan rat-killers, stable dogs who come along with the imported Irish dressage horses my niece has been training. "Tipperary Terriers," was the answer when I asked what kind they were.

Okay, I work in a library, a dog-positive library, where we have Sheba the service dog working in back most days, and where we have George the dog come in to listen to children read, and where most of us own beloved dogs, and where we have shelf after shelf of books about dogs; it should be easy to find something about these Tipperary Terriers and learn more about them.

I browsed the shelves. Turning straight to the index is an easy trick: no Tipperary Terriers, anywhere. Yeah, yeah, there's the Internet, and you get someone whose personality is compared to a Tipperary Terrier's, and other people casting about to find these dogs. I pulled a book from the shelf, opened it, and fell back. It's *Dogs: The Ultimate Dictionary of Over 1,000 Dog Breeds,* by Desmond Morris.

And there, though from its information I could only deduce the probable lineage of my sister's dogs, I forgot all about that project. I was introduced to ineffable treasure. There are fish-herding dogs. There is the Norwegian Puffin Dog. It turns out that my own dog, some kind of a McNab from Sonoma County, has the background of a cross between an extinct Scottish sheepdog called a Fox Shepherd and a Spanish sheepdog.

I fell further into the book. Fish-herding dogs? Yes. And not only do they leap into the water from the boat to herd the fish into the nets, they'll move the nets, catch escaping fish, and act as lookouts to bark alarms when shoals of fish are spotted. Then when fog descends, they become canine foghorns to warn other boats against collision, with their odd rising-and-falling barks.

Norwegian Puffin Dogs? You'll hardly believe it. These coastal Arctic dogs have an extra toe on each large paw for improved climbing grip, forelegs which will bend sideways at a 90° angle and a double-jointed neck for crawling into tight crevices, and ears which will fold over when necessary to protect against freezing rain. Their job? They climb up cliffs, wedge themselves into clefts in the rock, then dig into puffins' burrows, seize puffin fledglings, extricate themselves from the crannies, climb down, and deliver the birds to their owners, unharmed. Some of these dogs could procure as many as 80 birds in one hunting trip.

I kept reading, and kept reading, and eventually determined that what this book is about isn't just dogs. It's about human history, and what we've had to do to live, and how we've had the benefits of being in a symbiosis with these dog people for at least 10,000 years.

All revealed at the library. In just one book, a book open to all, discovered almost by accident, such marvels are found. And what's in the next book on the shelf? And the next one?

Lucinda Sahm deLorimier is a professional storyteller and Children's Librarian for the Nevada County Library

Good Dogs, Good Books

KATE DWYER

AT THE open-hearted age of eight, I wanted my own dog in the worst way. It was an impossibility for a girl who was still not reliably making her own bed, and already living in a house with a cranky, middle-aged dachshund. "You already have a dog," mother would say, looking at Schultz. "But I want my own dog," I would say, "one I can train and who will go on all my adventures with me, and be my best friend." Schultz bit children who tried to nuzzle their faces up against his. He hated adventures. Especially ones out in weather. He started ducking behind the couch whenever I came looking for him.

Mom was a resourceful woman. One day she walked me down to the children's entrance of the public library and, with the help of the librarian, pointed out a row of books. "Look," she said, "dogs." The best-trained, smartest, most devoted, most heroic dogs that ever lived, it turned out. Dogs that had done such amazing things they had become the subjects of whole books. The librarian recommended that, if I was dog crazy, I should read Jim Kierkegaard. Start with *Big Red*. It had dramatic scenery, a bachelor woodsman, capable and respectful of his dog, and a handsome Irish Setter who, of course, went everywhere with him.

After *Big Red*, I attacked the additional two feet of shelf space that Jim Kierkegaard's novels took up. Each featured another self-reliant outdoorsman and another gifted dog: a black Labrador named Buck; King, the fiercely loyal Husky; Jack, a vigilant and powerful German Shepard; Gipper, the dazzling Border Collie, who worked until his paws bled. All this research offered my parents a significant respite from my pleading. How could I get a dog until I knew which kind of dog I wanted? How could I know which dog I wanted until I'd read all the Jim Kierkegaard in the library? Schultz appreciated the hiatus too. I quit trying to wedge him into the basket of my bicycle for the outings he never enjoyed. How could he? His delicate feet slipped through the wire basket with each bump, the winter wind penetrated him through both his sweater and his short, shedless coat. And he knew the girl pedaling would have huge expectations of him, once they stopped, thanks to Jim Kierkegaard.

I panicked months later when I came to the last book on the shelf and asked the librarian if Mr. Kierkegaard had written a new book yet, because I was almost done with all the dog/man books. She smiled her calm, bodhisattva smile, then offered me my next key to the universe, a lesson in how the card catalogue worked. I might be done with Jim Kierkegaard, but look! We still have all these other cards under D for Dog. Did I want to read more dog novels, or would I like to read some "non-fiction" books about dogs and how to train them, and what people use them for, and why certain breeds do certain things and other breeds do other things? I was stunned with the potential of this new tool. I could find everything here. All kinds of questions and curiosities never addressed in school—and the building was open every night. It was open on Saturdays and Sunday afternoons. It seemed the most powerful invention of all time; a building full of books about everything, that is never closed. The world split wide open. Anything was possible—even for a little girl on a bike, with a disgruntled dachshund in her basket.

At 11, the yellow Labrador puppy of my dreams finally arrived in my Christmas stocking, and I became my own Jim Kierkegaard novel, exploring the world with a dog who could run beside my bicycle as I meandered the country roads around the edge of town, turning them into the wilds of the Great North Woods on one outing and the Red Rock Canyons of Southern Utah on the next. We stalked mice and rats like big game through silos of corn and soybeans. We were grand explorers, combing east central Illinois for every scrap of adventure it could parse out.

And once a week we pedaled downtown to the library. My dog would guard the bike rack while I wandered the shelves, looking for a new book to pry the top of my brain open and let more of the world in. Sometimes it was right on the front table, sometimes it was deep in a back room, but it was always there waiting ... dare I say it? Like a good dog.

Kate Dwyer lives on the San Juan Ridge

the only quiet moment is before I open the library

ROO CANTADA

still cold
sanctuary
comes to life
with the flick
of light switch, sign
heater fan
whirring.
within seconds
silence shattered
eager heads pop in
are you here? they ask
I peek out from behind the
picture book stacks
you are here!
I grin
nuh-uh!, stick out my tongue
then they are here
all of them choosing to
stay in the library for recess
milling about me like wild geese
pecking and chattering
no silence in my library
(I gave that idea up long ago)
busy little mouths, eager brains
now learning new computers
searching they are always searching
are dragons an animal they ask
find me a book, they say

after school,
my community spills out,
makes its way to our little campus,
preschoolers toddle about
while emails soar at

unheard of Ridge speed
wow! daddies exclaim in wonder
can I print, mommies ask.
I flit from child to adult, and back to child
showing off our fairy tales,
our perma-culture, our new fiction
like precious jewels or fine paintings
have you seen this? or this?
I present proudly
this is my dream job
I am constantly smiling
and never silent
in my library

Roo Cantada is the Twin Ridges School librarian and is the former co-host of Radio Poets Society on KVMR

Castle. *Pencil drawing by Linda Neely*

Closing In

PATRICIA BLACK

I GOT my first library card at the age of ten, after our family moved to a town with a good library. My parents were both readers, so my sister and I grew up with very good models to follow. At the library was an endless supply of books, all waiting to be taken home by me. It was like being led to a gold mine.

But I really learned about libraries by working in one. With a degree in Art I became the Assistant in the Marquand Library at Princeton University, a collection of books on art, architecture, and archaeology. There I met faculty members who had written some of the texts I'd used in my art classes. Beautiful old rare books, many handwritten on vellum, were kept in the "cage" behind a locked jail-cell door. The year was 1954, and our shelver, Mr. Wooden, was a retired Princeton alumnus of the class of 1907. He had his own recipe for a special concoction to soften and nourish old leather bindings. What it really did was make the leather-bound books stick together on the shelves, but my boss couldn't bring herself to tell him. Mr. Wooden also spent time concealed in the stacks snoozing or reading the paper, but nobody minded.

At Stanford University, where I worked for twenty-one years in news and publications, I had the opportunity to write profiles of librarians. That is where I learned that they are consumed with curiosity. They know a lot, but there is nothing a librarian cannot find out, and to see one of them closing in on his or her prey is a true joy.

Patricia Black lives on the San Juan Ridge

The Long and Winding Road to Becoming a Librarian

JUDY MARIUZ

NOT surprisingly, many of my earliest memories revolve around books and reading. I can still recall hopping on my bicycle as an eight-year-old and biking two miles to the public library to load up my bicycle basket with books. My bicycle, my library card, and ten cents for penny candy were all I needed to enjoy a perfect summer day. At home, I would pull out a folding lawn chair, find a spot in the back yard and dig into my pile of Nancy Drew mysteries while I watched the thunderclouds crawl across the darkening sky.

In seventh grade I joined the Library Club at school, and soon found myself volunteering as a "page" at the local library. The following summer I was offered a job (at seventy cents an hour) shelving books. Back in those days, everything was done by hand. I must have spent hours filing cards in the card catalog. I also got a chance to "mend" books with broken spines and listen to the middle-aged ladies gossip about their lives.

In high school I recall looking at the library director, Miss Farrell, a typical "spinster" of 55 with white curly hair. I remember feeling sorry for her, and thinking my life would never be like that. During my college years, I experienced libraries on a grander scale. Thanks to a generous scholarship, a student loan, and good grades, I was able to attend a prestigious Eastern women's college where the library was housed in a huge gothic-style building, and the reading room was furnished with overstuffed chairs and couches. Reading tables and study carrels were available for the more disciplined, but I spent most of my afternoons curled up in those cozy chairs.

While on a college exchange program during my junior year, I had the good fortune to meet the director of the Williams College Library in Williamstown, Massachusetts. He was impressed with my diligence performing a tedious task assigned to me as a work-study student. I can still recall him saying how unusual it was to find a bright student who would take on such a menial task and approach it with such industriousness. That encounter led to an offer of a summer job, and subsequently to an offer of full-time employment.

Then there was the day a few months later when my boyfriend came to tell me that my father had just died of a sudden heart attack. Unfortunately, not all of my library memories have been happy ones.

The decision to become a librarian was a fairly natural one for me. I had always loved to read, and I thought library science would be the perfect occupation for someone with a variety of interests who couldn't settle on just one. It was also a "cool" profession to choose back in the mid-seventies. The low salaries that librarians traditionally earn was one way of eschewing a culture of money and materialism. But that decision became decidedly less "cool" as the reality of supporting myself set in. Still, reading is undeniably one of the most inexpensive forms of entertainment available, and I have never regretted developing such a portable, enlightening and entertaining "hobby."

Life as a single middle-aged librarian is not at all what my youthful impression of Miss Farrell led me to expect. I get to spend my days immersed in the world of books and ideas, while discreetly checking out the attractive male patrons who occasionally wander in. Librarians provide a valuable service, while meeting all sorts of people and becoming recognizable faces in the small communities where we live. The library is my "home away from home" and my co-workers are like my family. We laugh, we squabble, we tease, we provide support to each other and we commiserate when we're feeling overworked and underpaid.

Living the life of a librarian is anything but boring. Each day brings a new question, a new book, an occasion for humor, and an opportunity to contribute to an important institution. Libraries are a gateway to knowledge and an equalizer of opportunities. They represent all that is admirable and worthwhile about our country and our society. Freedom of expression, creativity, a forum for opposing points of view, a sharing of resources and knowledge, as well as people working together to make the community a better place. I'm so proud to be a librarian and so grateful for the path that brought me here.

Judy Mariuz is the Librarian of the Grass Valley Royce Branch

Misreading
CATHERINE ALLEN

I LIKE most librarians, but there's one I remember from not so long ago who was not nice. Whenever I got her in the checkout line, which seemed to be almost always, she never failed to scold and shame me about overdue books. She somehow made me feel like I had dirty hands or a runny nose. I found no sympathy for her.

One day she wasn't there, and then the next. My experience at the checkout counter became comfortable again, friendly even. I had never been very late with books in the first place.

One day I commented to the librarian that I really enjoyed her attitude and asked "whatever happened to the librarian from hell?" She smiled at me, agreeing with the obvious—the other librarian was rude and unkind and it was a relief to have her gone.

Months later I found out that she had died from a brain tumor that had been the cause of the personality changes I had witnessed. At first I felt shame, but it was quickly replaced by sadness—sadness that she had been so misread and misunderstood during her last days in this library.

Catherine Allen lives in Nevada City

Part III. Anything Can Happen

My Second World

M. M. JOHNSON

IN MY childhood, that lovely stone building on Pine Street in Nevada City was the center of my universe. Grandma Nell lived on South Pine Street and Aunt Alice on North Pine and my own home was on Coyote, the next street over. My grammar school was just up the hill from the library and my dad's garage business was down where the freeway now cuts through old Main Street. These bounded my wanderings but the library was a door to all the world. I had no idea that the building was a gift from the richest man in the world, a far-off person with a philanthropic turn of mind in his old age.

Precocious in my reading and, as an only child, pushed by loneliness to read by the hour, I devoured literature of all sorts. Some were certainly unsuitable: I remember reading *The Odyssey* in 1940 while in the third grade, wondering about that cyclops eating the men and being killed by a heated stake driven into his one terrible eye. I read *Lorna Doone* that year too.

The next year our life changed when World War II was abruptly thrust on us. My father more or less disappeared into lots of extra work, Mother was gone a lot also, and reading the *Reader's Digest* and *The Saturday Evening Post* cover-to-cover wasn't nearly enough. I was in and out of the library on every trip across my "territory." I even tried to learn French, so as to expand my choices, but soon discovered that the syntax was different and gave up. I found I couldn't just memorize the different words and plug them in!

One book that fascinated me was *The Year is a Round Thing* by Helene Davis. Imagine my surprise when Mother said she knew the author; would I like to meet her? Would I! Mrs. Davis was from Norway but had married an American engineer. Mom set up a nice afternoon with her friend in her beautiful home on Boulder Street. For a nine-year-old bookworm, it was unforgettable to take tea with her and listen to more tales in her soft Norwegian accent.

The book told of her childhood in Tromsö, a seaport north of the Arctic Circle, where long dark winters closed in and people moved through snow tunnels from house to house. Stories of holidays as they were celebrated around the circle of the year, with Christmas at the top, made an interesting theme to follow, punctuated by folk tales. "The Droog," a huge ghostly fisherman who appeared when seamen were in danger, was the subject of one such story. Helene had seen the Droog one night and the men rushed off to the rescue. A child ran sobbing to tell them that a boat with its men had gone down.

Other stories were softer and included one of her mother playing Beethoven's Moonlight Sonata on the piano after Helene and her sister went up to their beds. I was amazed: it had never occurred to me that just as we played such classics in our family, so did other people in far countries. A Norwegian mother at the piano in a dark unrelenting winter, her children listening above, warm in their beds, made me feel my world had spread out and now included everybody.

Today there is a bigger library, still close to me, for I'm living in the old family home on Coyote Street, and it is just a bit uphill by the Nevada County Center. Occasionally the old site has a book sale down on its basement sidewalk and my children and grandchildren go by and browse. Inside the building is a research museum, named for Doris Foley, one of my teachers in that nearby grammar school, in which 1 have found many an interesting fact about our pioneer family. From their times to ours, the libraries have been a great part of our lives.

M. M. Johnson lives in Nevada City

Doris Foley Library in Nevada City. *Painting by Loana Beeson*

Summers at the Library

CATHY WILCOX-BARNES

DURING interminably long hot summer days my sister and I would hurry through our chores. One hour pulling horehound in the pasture, one hour working on the yard, one hour cleaning the barn, one hour weeding in the garden. At last we were free for the rest of the day. The oppressive heat of summer would bear down on us as we traveled the one-mile distance from our house to town. We were usually barefoot, money being extremely scarce in our house, or we wore flip-flops (bought two for a dollar at the Sav-Mor Variety Store on Broad Street). We'd hop-scotch our way toward town, running from one slim patch of shade cast by a telephone pole to another. Stopping meant feet sticking to tarry patches on the pavement.

A quick stop at the Alpha Hardware for a drink of water, then one last push up North Pine Street. At last, we'd reach our destination—the cool sanctuary of the Nevada City Library. Just walking through the front door brought instant relief. It wasn't that it was air-conditioned, in fact I suspect it wasn't. But the world inside was magical to me. The lemon-oil smell of the wooden tables, the shelves and shelves of books beckoning. I'd slowly run my finger over each book in the section I'd chosen for that day, waiting for just the right title to call to me or the right look or feel of the book. I'd select several books and carry them back to the chair by the window. When I looked out and up I'd see the jail window where Grandpa Martz would sometimes be waiting to wave to me. He was the Chief of Police in Nevada City at the time and always seemed to spend more time up at the jail than down at City Hall.

After an hour or two, we'd select our three books, the maximum we were allowed to check out at one time. Just before a weekend the librarian (I can't seem to recall her name right now, but she was Percy Crosswhite's sister) would let us check out four. We always had them back before the due date, because we wouldn't have been able to pay the three-cent fine for being late, and the thought of having our library card canceled was terrifying.

The summer I was seven or eight, I worked my way through the Bobbsey Twins and the Happy Hollisters. I can still remember them being located on the left-hand side of the library, back wall, two shelves down. When I was ten my mother became ill and we'd select books for her to read to us as she lay on her bed. Those were the years of *Goodbye*

My Lady, Tarzan, Peter Pan, National Velvet, and the Nancy Drew series. Sometimes when Mom was not feeling up to reading, I'd read to her. Those were really special times, escaping the pain and misery of our world together through books.

My mother died in the Spring just before the Summer I turned 13. That was the year I discovered a new section: "Classics for Juniors." I zealously worked my way through *Ivanhoe, The House of the Seven Gables, Return of the Native,* and many other wonderful works. I'd think to myself, *Mom would have liked this one.* I should have realized that with her love for books she'd probably read them all before she died.

As the summers passed, my tastes in books changed but my taste for books never did. I had a voracious appetite. I was addicted! I still am!

Cathy Wilcox-Barnes is the former City Clerk of Nevada City and a member of the Nevada City Rotary Club.

Miss Pickerel Goes to Mars

MARIA BROWER

I GREW up in and around Los Angeles during the 1950s. My parents divorced when I was not quite six. We moved a lot, and by the time I graduated from Los Angles High School in 1964 I had attended twelve schools in Los Angeles County, two of them twice! This disruption of my early education, usually in the middle of a semester, was probably the reason I was shy and introverted throughout most of my childhood. I was an only child those first six years, and until after my mother's second marriage I spent my early years primarily with adults. My mother read to me very early from the popular Little Golden Books. I was able to recite my favorites from memory before entering school and learning to read myself.

My mother married again, and I soon had a baby brother, and years later a sister. I wasn't neglected, but my mother was busy with the little ones, I was in school most of the day, and she didn't have time to read to me. My salvation came from my introduction to the public library and what would become a life-long love of books. In the 3rd grade Miss Gorsksey's class from Hobart Elementary School went on a field trip to the public library. Here I discovered a friendly haven, a peaceful book-filled world, where I learned I could experience many adventures.

My early favorites from that time period were by timeless authors: Laura Ingalls Wilder, Louisa May Alcott, and a series of books about an older grandmother-type lady who had adventures which included my favorite, *Miss Pickerel Goes to Mars* by Ellen MacGregor. From that time on I was an avid library user, and after entering Mt. Vernon Junior High School I chose Library Service as my elective. This helped me to become familiar with a wide range of topics, non-fiction, and the Dewey Decimal System.

Today I work and manage the local history branch of the Nevada County Library, the Doris Foley Library for Historical Research. I am fortunate to work in this beautiful 1907 Carnegie Library building in Nevada City among a world of wonderful books. It is rewarding to have adults come in and reminisce about using this library as a child, and how it still looks and even smells the same. Not only do I have the joy of discovering old book "treasures" here that I have not yet read, but I am also able to introduce patrons to these books, assist with their research needs, and help them to solve mysteries and find treasures of their own.

On my vacations and travels I visit many public and research libraries across the country. I have done research on two islands of Hawaii and in many State Libraries and Archives in the Mid-Atlantic region and, in comparison, Nevada County has an impressive local history collection. Nevada County is immersed in history and supported by its residents, because the people who choose to live here appreciate its rich heritage.

Maria Brower is the former Branch Manager of the Doris Foley Library for Historical Research in Nevada City

Dappled Light in the Linden Trees; Doris Foley Library.
Graphite pencil drawing by Suzanne Olive, Nevada City

When my sons, now eighteen and twenty, were little I would take them to our local library, the Doris Foley Library in Nevada City, to join with other children listening to stories. My sons and I would often sit outside on the retaining wall and look up at the dappled light in the leaves of the giant Linden trees. The old stone building with the intimate spaces and beautiful shade trees was a welcoming first library for my sons. This was a special place and time. —*Suzanne Olive*

Blessings

TOM TAYLOR

I THINK I was 11 the first time I ventured into the Nevada City Public Library with dignified purpose. Mrs. Billick, stern Duchess of the Sixth Grade, had assigned research reports with footnotes and bibliography (what are those?) of staggering length on a country of choice. My cross was Spain. I can still recall the green outline of Iberia on my labored map of geography and resources—a star for Madrid, the lozenge of Portugal—with mountains and rivers, iron ore and wheat, resplendent in excess color and detail. Our house had lots of books, but nothing on Spain other than Compton's *Pictured Children's Encyclopedia*, circa 1913, handed down to my mother as a girl. It was sort of interesting about Elevators and what the Woodsman told Johnny about Beavers, but its angle on history was ancient and creepy. I was embarrassed for my parents, who were quite literate but too stingy to acquire respectably current reference works for their hungry children. That's what the library is for, they said. Aha. So off I trudged with my binder and their benediction, at least at first.

The library seemed bigger then, but little has changed other than its name and purpose—now the Doris Foley Library for Historical Research, a registered National Historic Landmark (ahem). It perches in compact gravity on the corner knoll below the Courthouse, flanked by terraced majesty of lindens and maples, a vaulted bower of cooling descent in summer and spectacular glory in autumn. They were planted shortly after the edifice was dedicated in 1907, funded in 1904 by the Carnegie Endowment—notes the plaque—courtesy of Andrew Carnegie, King of Steel, richest man in the world. He amassed his swag on the backs of legions, but attention must be paid to the 3,000 libraries his booty made.

Shiver of glass as the door latch clicks closed, creak up the wide stairs, arid stale musk of wood, vellum, paper, ink... perfume of history. Step up into the chapel clustered with saga and lore, teeming stacks of data and argument awaiting their turn in democratic hush, measured by tick tock of the grandfather clock, metronome of silence, knelling the hours. The high-backed occasional chairs and rocker are scuffed with age, but testify to sturdy grace and durable craft of men long dead. There was usually a pleasant lady with gray curls behind the broad checkout desk who processed books and shushed eruptions. I was rudely incurious about her name, but she had my number. By my third or fourth landing in conquest of Spain her smile of greeting had cooled.

That first ascent was innocent. But as I turned to the great table, there lurked a cohort of my classmates, Sarah, presiding. She was smart, sassy—and subversive. I was abashed but thrilled to be the lone boy among whispered intrigues of insurgent girls in captured territory.

Ssshhh! went the lady. Tick. Tock.

Sarah knew the terrain and directed me to the candidate shelves. Encyclopaedia Brittanica ... who reads this? Colliers? hmm. Try the World Book. Bingo. Here was modern stuff in straight prose I could groom to my own, illustrations and *MAPS*—but way too much. I copied with abandon, editing here and there to detune the style, leapfrogging vast acres of text with glib summary, pulling direct quotes at random for my footnotes. It should have taken two visits at most, but I went twice that for the spice, until the parents got wise and reeled me in. I bargained for one more visit to finish my "research," which meant grabbing a vanity from the Brittanica for the illusion of a second source, before the agony of a clean rewrite. I tried to weasel my mother into typing it, but no dice. I went nuts with the map.

Mrs. Billick rewarded my guile with an A and a warm compliment. I doubt if she was fooled, but it had the required elements and bulk. I think Sarah got an A+. She probably typed hers, and it had graphs or something—in addition to a map.

Some years ago, after my mother died, I was cleaning out her basement and *SPAIN, Land of Contrasts* surfaced. I was stunned. Something nudged me to smell it and I got a waft of the library stairs mixed with her scent, which summoned the rest of it. You can't Google that.

Tom Taylor lives in Nevada City

Finding Me in the Library

CHRIS OLANDER

THE year 1972 began my two sons' school education. I read books to them that they checked out from their school library, books they wanted to hear. I had always read stories to them at bedtime, using dramatic enthusiasm with animation to open their imaginations. My sons asked me to come to their classes, first and second grades, and read for story time; their teachers were boring readers. I began a weekly reading stint in their classes; soon, I graduated to a story hour in the library: three class session of 45 minutes, two sessions each Thursday. I found my calling—my children led me to it.

Fall 1978, I entered Saint Martin's College, majoring in English –Drama–Psychology. My junior and senior years, I worked in the library. I read between checking books out and in. Most students traveled across town to the modern metal-shelved, spacious Evergreen State College Library for the newest slick-covered books. I enjoyed isolated carrels, window-lit, in dark recesses among cavernous shelves of old cloth-vintages, out-of-vogue editions, which had been replaced by post-modern revisionists across town.

Saint Martin's library was the original wood, built in 1880s—but funky: scratched, stained, varnish peeling off neglected ancient hardwoods. In undisturbed silent reveries, I discovered new heroes: Roderick Nash, *Wilderness and the American Mind*; Whitman's *Leaves of Grass*; Ralph Waldo Emerson's poetry and essays; Thoreau's *Walden*. I found my people in a quiet wooden sanctuary, a gold mine of wisdom in a red brick college building called Old Main, Olympia, Washington.

From 1986 till 1991, I was resident janitor at the Nevada City Library on North Pine Street. I had the keys to wealth Monday and Thursday, all night, till it opened at ten AM the next day. Mop floors; dust desks, counters, and wood work; vacuum carpets—then, real work: writing and revising my poetry. On the circulation desk (a wooden classical design donated by the city in the 1960s) I spread my papers, working magic in words and meanings, conjuring poetic epiphanies: *Library Poems, 1986 to 1991*.

A beautiful library, silver cinder-block-built, dedicated October 4, 1907, from Andrew Carnegie's wealth, well-stocked with essential knowledge—access to resources in Grass Valley's Library and statewide. All wood original shelves; tapered, classical wood columns supported the arched ceiling's central room; elegant decorative molding, stylish black and white linoleum squares hints Surrealistic Royalty! I dusted and polished wooden sheens; 19 windows eight feet high, three feet wide, provided light in the darkest days. Venetian blinds I cleaned once; "haven't been cleaned since," says the present librarian. Here I typed 20 student poetry anthologies from Placer, Sierra, and Nevada county schools where I taught poetry writing; five Empire H. S. anthologies, six Nevada Union H. S. anthologies.

Behind the circulation desk, reciting my newest bardic creation, sometime after midnight, in early spring, a door slammed in the basement! Quiet! I continued reciting. Steps climbing the stairway frightened me to pause. Who was rising from below? Madelyn Helling! Head Librarian! She enters the room.

"Oh, Hi!" I blurted, embarrassed.

"Well," she said slowly. "That's an interesting poem you were reading. You certainly have a lively style and strong voice. Very good—is it yours?"

"Yeah!" I blushed. "Was it too loud?" I asked, awkwardly gathering up my papers and supplies as if preparing to leave.

"No, not at this hour. I saw lights on, thought I'd check." She paused, reflecting, then, "Yes, libraries are the centers for culture and literature in a community." She smiled at me. "Good night, lock the doors!" descended the stairway and left.

Would I get fired? Had I overstepped the boundaries for art on county property and time? A few weeks later, Jeremiah Raven asked me to participate in a poetry reading at the old library to help raise money for the proposed new library. Accepted for mining my gold from a historic gold mining town's historic library, I had become a poet!

At the Library Benefit reading, "Poet's Salute to the Old Library," May 17, 1991, many of us—Jeremiah Raven, John Barbato, Joy Phillips, Jody Lynn Hughes, Tim McHarque, Chris Olander—read poetry, songs and stories. We had a great time of it: drank a little wine with refreshments, a who's who gracious audience, good talk, heady enthusiasm for the new Madelyn Helling Library. Ahh! The honor: contributing poetry to fund a community's library, a center for knowledge, ideas and expression: freedom through wisdom.

Chris Olander is a Nevada City poet and performer

My Favorite Place in Nevada County

JULIAN EISEN

HAVE you ever befriended a wild mustang? Is your best friend a witch? Has a bomb ever landed near *your* house? All of these things have happened to me in my favorite place in Nevada County.

Now let me tell you a little more about the things I've done in my favorite place. I have been saved from a rabid dog by a young bear hound. I've been shipwrecked with my family and stranded on a remote island.

My dog once saved me from a pack of wild boars! He was hurt very badly, so I ran home and got my mom. When we got to him, we cleaned him up and stitched his wounds closed with tail hairs from our mule. Then we got a big piece of hide from the saddle bags, tied ropes to it, and the mule carried him home. Luckily he was better in a few weeks. He was my hero!

I have slain dragons and ogres. I have fought a giant and won; but the next day its brother with two heads came to fight me—I won again. Another brother came each day and each one had one more head than the one from the previous day. They did not die until all of their heads were removed. The last giant had 20 heads!

I've traveled across the universe on a mission to bring peace to all galaxies. I volunteered at Pearl Harbor to search for survivors. I have befriended Nevada's legendary stallion, the Phantom.

I even saved a draft horse from the slaughter house. To repay me, he kept me safe in an earthquake; then helped release other horses that were trapped in the barn when it caved in.

I bet you're wondering what my favorite place could be. Can you guess? Anything can happen in my favorite place in Nevada County—it's the Madelyn Helling Library.

When I open a book, I fall inside. Anything can happen.

Julian Eisen, Nevada City, 11 years old

A Case of Mistaken Identity

DICK PHILLIPS

During 1990 I had been frequently driving to Nevada County's Eric Rood County Government Center when both the Madelyn Helling Library and the jail were being built on the same property. The building on the left was large and very imposing. The one on the right up the hill was rather modest.

I paid virtually no attention to these two buildings until one day when I was asked to attend a meeting in the conference room of the Library. Without a second thought I drove up there, turned left and pulled up right in front of the entrance to the big building—only to look up and see that the lettering above the door said Wayne Brown Correctional Center.

What a shock that was! Imagine that criminals get bigger and better quarters than the treasured wealth of mankind—our books.

Yes, I did go to the meeting in the little building on the hill, but I was so angry at the obvious imbalance in our society that will I never forget the experience.

Dick Phillips of Grass Valley is on the Nevada County Library Foundation Board

My First Library Encounter

EDWIN L. TYSON

I REMEMBER well my very first encounter with a library some eighty years ago, and how that was the beginning of what I refer to as my lifetime reading binge.

I grew up in a large house on a huge farm in northwest Missouri surrounded by parents, grandparents, aunts and uncles, and various frequent guests, all of whom would take time to read to a child with a book. Books were frequent gifts for birthdays and Christmas and were always around. We received two daily newspapers, *The Kansas City Star* and the *St. Joseph News-Press*, as well a numerous magazines such as *Collier's, The Saturday Evening Post, American Magazine*, and five or six women's magazines, all of which contained serial fiction.

At the age of five I started school in a one-room schoolhouse with fourteen or fifteen pupils in the eight grades. It was there that I first encountered "the library." It was a large cabinet of shelves filled with books behind two glass doors. There that at the age of eight I discovered a translation of *The Iliad*. That began my reading binge from which I have never recovered. Emily Dickinson was so right when she suggested there's no frigate like a book.

During the mile walk across an open bluegrass pasture between home and school I imagined taking part in all those highly romantic battles between the Greeks and the Trojans on the plains of Troy. And I was fascinated by the way those gods and goddesses manipulated and interfered with the affairs of mortal men.

My never-ending love affair with Shakespeare began when I entered high school. Since our curriculum called for reading only one Shakespeare each year, it was the library that provided access to all the plays as well as the sonnets. During World War II, friends used to gather round to watch when I packed for our move to the next South Pacific island. In addition to all the GI stuff we had to carry, I had to make room for a volume of *The Complete Works of Shakespeare*, a collection of the overseas editions of *The New Yorker*, and numerous paperbacks such as *The Collected Works of Robert Frost, Moby Dick*, etc.—my library away from home.

After the war and a bit of graduate study at the University of California I became a teacher of English at a Bay Area high school. It was there that I learned just how necessary a good library and a good librarian are to any school curriculum. It was this realization that influenced my decision to enroll in the School of Librarianship at the University of Washington. Upon graduation I returned to the high school where I had been an English teacher for years and was allowed to work with the architects on plans for a new library. The end result was magnificent.

Not long after that I moved to San Jose City College as head reference librarian, and taught a course in Basic Reference Materials and Services at San Jose State University for the next fourteen years until I retired.

The move to Nevada City thirty years ago didn't mean leaving libraries. Since my arrival here I've been involved with the Searls Historical Library of the Nevada County Historical Society. I started as a volunteer one afternoon a week. That grew to two days, and then three. Finally, when Doris Foley, the one chiefly responsible for the existence of the historical library, became ill, I was placed in charge. There was a period of five or six years when I worked six afternoons a week. Fortunately, I now have some excellent volunteers who are also interested in libraries and library services, and I'm down to three afternoons weekly.

At the age of eighty-eight I'm still a read-a-holic. My house is filled with books, I check books out at our County Library every two weeks, and I subscribe to too many magazines and newsletters. I frequently go three or four days without turning the television or radio on. Talk about self-indulgence.

Edwin L. Tyson has worked for many years at the Searls Historical Library in Nevada City

Searls Law Office. *Lithographic drawing by George Mathis*

The Library of Peter van der Pas

PRISCILLA VAN DER PAS

WHEN I first met Peter around 1980 and heard that he had a fabulous library, I was intrigued by the idea of an individual owning his own library. Why would anyone want to have his own when there were public libraries everywhere?

Peter's "Pacific Library" was located at St. Joseph's Cultural Center in Grass Valley. In 1977 he and Molly had moved from South Pasadena to Grass Valley. Searching for towns to retire in, a prospective location for the library was more important than finding a house to live in, and a suitable location was the basement of St. Joseph's. A whole moving van carried the approximately 10,000 boxes of books from Pasadena to their new home in Grass Valley. They themselves found a small house across town. Peter took his daily walk to the library, unpacking and arranging his books. Soon they began to organize book displays and various types of programs for the public.

It was during one of these public events that I first visited the library, and it was truly impressive! Peter would encourage people to wander in the aisles, browsing over whatever they found interesting. People discovered they couldn't read some of the books because many were in French, German, or Dutch, all of which Peter could read and write. There were also many Japanese botanical drawing and painting books. (Peter never learned to speak Japanese, but he had reference books to look up characters for interpretation.)

Molly became ill with cancer. Slowly her life came to an end in 1983, and Peter was on his own. Since Peter had lost an eye during World War II, he had never driven, so I often drove him places. We became more than friends, and married in 1984. Gradually I learned how he had acquired his library. (He never finished his love of acquisition of new books, for until shortly before his death in 2003 he was still ordering books!)

This is what Peter once wrote about how he began his own library:

> The origin of the collection goes back perhaps to the time I was about 12 years old. I was reading a popular book on natural history, and the author wrote about a certain Leeuwenhoek without explanation, as if everyone knew all about him. I had never heard of the man and the assumption of the author that I should have, disturbed me very much. I decided to find out about Leeuwenhoek and other

Peter van der Pas in 1976. *Sacramento Bee photo by Skip Shulman.*

famous people. And I never forgot him; at the moment my Library has an excellent collection of the works of this early Dutch microscopist.

In my home town of Breda, Holland, there was an open air market on Fridays. I had to pass this market square on my way to and from school. There were always stalls where old books were sold. Buying fascinating old books, I got a valuable experience in dealing with market merchants. After high school, I went to Delft Institute of Technology, where there were also book merchants; I continued to add to my collection. Studying physics, I discovered that the writings of the people who had actually worked in physics were much more interesting than the textbooks I had to read.

During the German occupation of Holland from 1940 to 1945, many young Dutch men were sent to Germany to work camps. Since I had a job as lab assistant to a professor, I was fortunate enough to be able to stay at Delft and pursue my interest in other scientists, such as Ingenhousz, Mendel, and Hugo de Vries, so my collection grew.

As the Germans were retreating from Holland at the end of the war, Peter served in the British Army Bomb Disposal Corps, losing an eye.

Later he worked for the Dutch Shell Oil Company, who sent him to California. He married Molly, had three children, and worked for other oil companies. But he never got over his scientific interest, acquiring more books and writing scientific articles. The California History collection began after retiring to Grass Valley, when he became the editor of the Nevada County Historical Society *Bulletin* for 20 years, writing many articles himself.

After Peter died in December 2003, the library was dispersed. The scientific books went to Utah State University, the Dutch history collection to Hope College in Holland, Michigan, the California books to the Nevada County Historical Society's Searls Library, and the miscellaneous books to our Nevada County Library.

Nobody who knew Peter could think of him without associating him with his beloved Pacific Library. It was truly his lifetime occupation and his life's passion.

Priscilla van der Pas, of Grass Valley, has filled many offices in the Nevada County Historical Society

Note from Steve Fjeldsted: Not long ago I read a wonderful statement in *Thinking in Pictures* by Temple Grandin offering the notion that libraries contain our out-of-body genes because ideas are passed on like genetic traits. In this way, according to an official at New York Public Library who is represented in the book, libraries are a place where immortality is available because they contain the collective memory of humanity. The text goes on to report that Isaac Asimov's obituary contained his remark that death was not absolutely final for him because his thoughts would live on in his books, giving him a kind of immortality. Grandin further postulates that immortality might be the effect one's thoughts and actions can have on other people. One Nevada County individual who has left a treasure of thoughts and actions for future generations is Peter van der Pas.

On Keeping Books

A. J. LEIS

Rows of ideas upon the shelves,
We reach above, outside ourselves,

To hear the sounds of every age,
Weeping, and laughter, up from the page,

To know wisdom from folly and law from crime,
Which merge or converge with the passage of time,

To sense fragrant roses, the taste of bread,
The touch of a lover, the nod of a head,

To learn of nuts, and bolts, and family vacations,
How to build fences, and how to build nations,

To savor words and stories and beats of our hearts,
Through literature, poetry, history, arts,

The library bursts at its own seams,
Steward of these human dreams.

A. J. Leis lives in Chicago Park

Longing to Be Della Street

DEE MURPHY

I WAS in the second grade when I first discovered the library. There I was sitting criss-cross applesauce on the library floor of Hennessy School. Earlier that day my second grade teacher had finished reading an Encyclopedia Brown book to our class. Then she surprised us by announcing that we were going to visit the school library for the first time, and that we would be allowed to check out one book, and that we would be able to keep that book for a whole week.

We walked single file to the library where we listened to the hushed voice of the school librarian explaining the rules of library use. After the librarian told us to go find our book, my classmates fanned to all reaches of the library. I walked shyly up to the librarian and asked if she had the Encyclopedia Brown book my teacher had just finished reading. She smiled, and pointed me to an entire shelf of Encyclopedia Brown books. Forgetting the one-book rule, I immediately gathered all the Encyclopedia Brown books my seven-year old arms could carry and took them to the librarian. She kindly explained that I could only check out one book at a time. But, she informed me that just up the hill stood the Grass Valley Library, and that, if I wanted to, I could get a library card and check out as many books as I wanted. I also found out that I could go to the Grass Valley library every day, not just once a week. I had discovered library heaven.

The very next day after school, my mom walked with me up the concrete steps to the enormous white building which housed the Grass Valley Library. We opened the heavy doors, and I immediately felt at home. I loved the smooth, heavy, wooden tables and the hard chairs. I loved the musty smell, and the hush that wasn't quite silence. All I could hear were books being taken in and out of shelves, the sound of pages being turned, and the scrape of shoes and chairs against the wooden floor. When asked where the children's books were, the librarian pointed towards a staircase which led down to the basement. My mom and I crept down the staircase together. At the bottom of the stairs the narrow staircase opened into a large room filled with children's books of all kinds. I was stunned to discover another shelf of Encyclopedia Brown books just begging to be read. This time I was able to check out five Encyclopedia Brown books. And, if I finished reading them all in one night, I could come back the next day and check out five more!

My mom and I soon established a weekly routine where she would drop me off at the library while she would grocery shop at Safeway and run errands at Smiths Department Store (now part of the Safeway parking lot) and Sprouse-Reitz (now the Salvation Army Thrift Store). I always had at least one hour, or more, to browse and read through the children's book section before my mom came back to pick me up, her wood-paneled station wagon full of groceries. Eventually, the Grass Valley librarians began to know me by name, and they started giving me suggestions for other books I might like. Because of these kind and helpful women I discovered *Charlotte's Web* and *Little Women,* still today two of my favorite books of all time.

The librarians noticed that I had a penchant for mysteries, so they made recommendations that I try the Nancy Drew, the Hardy Boys, and Trixie Belden series of books. I devoured each book in no time. By the sixth grade, I had read every book I wanted to read in the children's section of the Grass Valley Library. The librarians decided I was ready to graduate to the adult fiction section upstairs. Thanks to them, I discovered Ellery Queen, Perry Mason (Oh, how I longed to be Della Street), and Alfred Hitchcock.

Even today, some 35 years later, you will find me browsing through the mystery fiction section of the Madelyn Helling Library. I am thankful every day for my love of reading, and I am grateful to those gracious librarians who helped me along the way.

*Dee Murphy of Grass Valley works for the
Nevada County Counsel's Office*

Josiah Royce Library, Grass Valley. *Painting by Loana Beeson*

Why I Like the Library

HAROLD BERLINER

MY first experience with libraries came when I was in the lower grades of grammar school. It was a necessity, because the school library didn't have enough material for my homework. But I soon found out that the books I needed were not the only thing. The library became a gathering place for children of my age, one of many such gatherings, going on simultaneously. We helped each other with homework, then just talked. The only rule was that we were quiet in our talking. This produced a spread of knowledge, and the ability to speak to others on topics beyond the weather or football and baseball.

When I was 12, I spent two years in Grass Valley for reasons of health. Only in the second year did I go to school. So I had a lot of time on my hands, and spent a great deal of it in the library where Miss Alma Popp reigned. She alone kept the work going, with plenty of silence. She was very kind to me, and I found the things I needed, on my own or with her help. It was a lovely place, and quite adequate in 1939 for the much smaller population of western Nevada County. Today we have a number of libraries in the system, but as the people move in we must keep up with their needs. Fortunately we have a librarian who looks ahead, making the library a place of learning beyond books and magazines.

Walking into the library one enters a special world; free from hustle, telephones, and insistent duties. The library is a whole world in itself. One can journey to the moon, or relax with a good book. What is a good book? It varies with the individual. It may be a new novel, old classic, mystery, science fiction, western or current events. And there's no one to tell you what kind of book you are going to like or force a choice.

Indeed you may change your own mind at any time, and switch from one kind of thing to another. With computers you may expand this special world into something far more specialized, information is available on every subject, and made by people with differing views, which you may use to make a different view all your own.

The library with its books and computers makes our rights under the First Amendment to the Constitution real. There may be different interpretations to let you see what you feel is best.

Then there are racks of newspapers and magazines from many places. They're all free, although once in a while we may have to wait for someone to finish an article he or she is interested in. But during that wait you have magazines on special subjects that interest you, but you could not reasonably subscribe for the one article you're looking for.

Most libraries have comfortable chairs, ample space, and provide a perfect opportunity to enjoy life in undisturbed pleasure.

Harold Berliner is a printer, type designer, and former District Attorney of Nevada County

Anything Can Happen. *Photograph by Linda Pearson*

For Laverne: Excerpts from Remarks at Her Memorial Service

PETER COLLIER

MY first memories of her have to do with baseball. Big John (her husband) and I met when we were appointed by the Nevada City Little League to coach The Expos, a team of boys 13–16, featuring, naturally enough, our own sons who were the same age. The Expos got killed the first year. We made the Bad News Bears look good. But at the end of our third and final season we wound up tied for first place with The Cubs. There was to be a playoff to decide the championship. John Junior was our best pitcher, but Little League rules said he could only pitch every seven days. He had pitched four days earlier, but the manager of the opposing team said that some of his best players were about to leave for family vacations so he was willing to waive the rules. We were killing them for the first several innings. It was John Junior's day; they couldn't even begin to hit him. Then, with the game half over, the other manager began whining about us breaking the rules and how John Junior should be taken out. He ran off and got the Little League president to back him. Stupidly, Big John and I agreed to take John Junior out. You know how this story ends: our team fell apart and we lost the game. I went home absolutely devastated.

I'm still in the land of catatonia at around five o clock when the phone rings. It was Laverne. "The hell with those jerks," she says, "let's go have pizza." We went to Citizens Pizza, our hangout at the time, and had pizza and beer. For the next couple of hours, Laverne absolutely ripped the opposing coach and the league officials for stealing the championship from us. She was so droll and so creatively nasty about our opponents that the whole thing started to seem funny. By the end of the evening we were all feeling pretty good and the Colliers had officially signed up for the war against jackasses Laverne waged all during the 25 years I knew her.

So my first point is that Laverne did not suffer fools gladly. My second is that while Laverne was fun to be with and had a lacerating wit, she also had a depth most of us never plumbed. She was, among other things, one of the toughest people I've ever known. I saw it most clearly when her daughter Stacy was killed tragically in a car accident in 1990. I've never seen anyone more devastated than Laverne. But as the weeks passed, those unbearable weeks, you could see her slowly take hold while everyone else got ever more deeply mired in grief. You could see her thinking to herself, *I've got to stop this slide. I've got to save the rest of my family.* Without ever forgetting it, she set her own heartbreak aside and began to draw John, John Jr. and ultimately the grandkids into a tight, protective circle, helping them get through their own long night and then guiding them toward the light. I've never seen anything like it.

Other things about Laverne. She made a great spice cake, the best I've ever tasted. She fought her way through breast cancer without even a hint of theatricality or self-pity. And she was a great dancer. I learned that when my son Andrew, who had been on the ill-fated Expos baseball team with John Junior, got married in San Francisco right after 9-11. John and Laverne didn't much like to go to events like this, but because it was us they came down for the wedding. At one point during the reception, when the music was fully cranked up, I looked up through my father-of-the-groom haze and saw them dancing. It was amazing. They were by far the best dancers on the floor, young or old—in perfect synch, fluid and rhythmic and light on their feet. They didn't dance apart, but holding hands as they flung each other out and brought each other back in gracious circles. As I watched them and thought about all they had been through and all they had overcome, I realized that they had gone beyond being merely husband and wife. These two people were mates. They knew exactly how to move together—on the dance floor and in life. Laverne was absolutely floating on air that night.

Laverne had a withheld quality. She was not profligate with her emotions. But she was a deeply and naturally compassionate person. A few years ago my daughter Cait, who had grown up with Stacy, was diagnosed with cancer. There came the day I had to tell Laverne. She cried out and tears immediately squirted out of her eyes as she grabbed me. There was not the slightest pause between the emotion and the reaction. It was one of the best hugs I ever got precisely because it was so absolutely authentic. Laverne was definitely someone you wanted guarding your back when the chips were down.

She had extremely good literary taste and a real intellectual curiosity. It's what made her such a good person for the library: she read a lot and thought about the things she read. Just before Christmas, Mary Jo and I went with her and John to see "The Last Samurai." Afterwards, we went to Lyons, as we always did after a night at the movies, for a little film criticism, gossip, and pie a la mode. Laverne didn't give "The Last

Samurai" a very good review. But she and I got to talking about an improbable reference the Tom Cruise character makes in the middle of this Japanese epic to the Battle of Thermopolyae. You know, that famous battle around 480 B.C. where Leonidas and his 300 Spartans stood off tens of thousands of Persians for several days, dying to the last man in a sacrifice that bought Greece time to repel the invasion. I mentioned that I'd read a great historical novel about Thermopolyae called *Gates of Fire*. It was exactly the kind of book Laverne loved. She immediately got it from the library and was reading it when she became too sick to read any more. Maybe it was fitting that this was her last book: after all, Laverne was a warrior herself. She fought her way through the deaths of Stacy and her brother Tom and through her own breast cancer by simply refusing to go down. I imagine her at the end of her own last battle, when she had fought as hard as she could and it was still was clear she was going to lose. I imagine her looking at what was coming in that unflinching way of hers and thinking to herself, *Okay, I can do this thing. I'm not afraid. Let's get on with it.*

Pulitzer Prize-winning writer Peter Collier lives Nevada City

Laverne Vaughan

Nana's Library

MARY VOLMER

FOR the eight years she lived with us my Nana needed two things to make her happy: baseball and books. While her baseball loyalties remained firmly with the Bash Brothers and the Oakland As, her reading loyalties were far less stringent. Larry McMurtry and Daniel Steel were close companions in my Nana's bookshelf. Crossword puzzles and *National Geographics* lounged haphazardly on the same nightstand, and on the shelf behind her bed lived a motley collection of historical fiction and each and every western Louis L'Amour put a pen to. Trashy romances were banished under the bed with the cigarettes we all pretended not to know about.

This collection wasn't a library in any traditional sense. Nana organized books by most recent use, or, in the case of the romances, by content. To a six-year-old with her first library card, Nana's collection carried no semblance of the order I'd only just discovered at the "real" library in Grass Valley. Beyond those white pillars that guarded the door, books stood in lines like good soldiers, on shelves three times my height. I sneezed book dust and an old man shushed me with a molting finger, then winked and grinned with too few teeth. The fairyland-voiced children's librarian hovered, helpful, but worried, as if the books themselves were her children. And the books! Each row carried hundreds of stories, created hundreds of worlds, explained thousands of mysteries. If Nana's books were worn, familiar pets, the "real" library was a zoo full of exotic animals from every corner of the world.

Still, in her library Nana could find any book she wanted in an instant, just like the librarian; and her library served as worthy a purpose as any I've wandered through since. Nana's books defined her as much as strong black coffee and stories of Tucson during the Depression. Her library, like the collection of colored vials in the medicine cabinet, was a balm for old age and an escape.

Nana read to escape the chill of our converted craft room, to cover the rasp of my granddad's breath in the twin bed next to her. Page after page, long into the night, while the dog snored and Granddad wheezed, she'd slip back to ranch times, knowing full well she'd never return to such hardship given the chance. Her books were a safe place, a familiar place; inside she found her youth again, her strength again, the rush of sex again. She smoked strong cigarettes, and loved strong men with years ahead of them before the stroke made them—made *him*—an angry, wizened infant. The stroke that made them both dependent on their headstrong daughter and her loving mandates. Aerobics?! More fiber?! Less grease?!

When sleep finally came to her, it always came mid-sentence. I'd creep downstairs to her room and find the reading light making a sharp incision in the morning. If the cover of the book I found resting on her chest featured twisting bodies and swirling titles in gold or scarlet, I'd let the light be and watch for a moment. Nana's eyes were open slits, crusted and dry. Her breath told me she slept, though I imagined later, after she'd passed, that even then she saw me. Even then she watched me watching her; loved me loving her.

If the cover was an innocuous brown, with a safe, block title, I'd reach up to click off the light and tiptoe out again. I never spoke to her about this. I never told anyone.

Now my own library bears a cluttered resemblance to Nana's. Organization is an afterthought. Books with bar-codes and books without, pile up in the order that I read them. Margaret Atwood beneath Wallace Stegner beneath Susan Straight. Cozy. If people live on in memory, my Nana too lives on here in the careful chaos of my own library. And once in a while I'll wake in the blue-black early morning; the reading light will be off when I'd thought I'd left it on; a book will be open on my chest. And I just might hear the sound of baseball in the distance, or catch a short jolt of nicotine. My team is the A's, but my radio is off. I don't smoke. I won't tell you what books I keep under my bed. I trust that Nana won't either.

Mary Volmer lives in Nevada County

Shelving

SUE CAUHAPE

With an armload of books, the librarian
scans leather and paper spines,
somber greens and grays

splashes of ribald red.
Volumes slide into their proper places
like obedient faces all in rows

ready to show-and-tell, each one
like a magic wardrobe where she watches
Scout walk Boo Radley back home,

the brave cowboy slide down a rope of sheets,
and Frankenstein's monster learn Arabic
undetected through the woodshed wall.

She feels Leaphorn scale a sandstone chimney
in a cloudburst and Doc's rage
as he sweeps up the laboratory floor.

Fragrant summer air wafts around her as
Deanna chases coyote tracks
through a libidinous Kentucky wood.

The cadence of Dylan's ode to his
thirtieth year unto heaven echoes in her ear
and the untuned piano rings

through a California gold camp.
Finishing her task, she chooses one with a gentle tug
and settles beneath the lamp.

Sue Cauhape works at the Truckee Library

One Afternoon in the Grass Valley Library

TODD CIRILLO

I watched you
flow
through the library
as if
singing a song.

I thought
how nice it would have been
to have known
the words.

Todd Cirillo is a Grass Valley poet

Part IV. The Day I Wandered In

The Library Book Sale

KELLY KOLAR VALIN

TIME is a funny thing. As a child, an hour can scarcely be endured. Summer vacation is endless. Days slowly melt into weeks, and a month is an eternity. So it was that we, my sister and I, eagerly awaited the first Saturday of every month. That was the day the entire family prepared for a journey of great adventure.

It all began with us piling into the car. After the important decisions of who was sitting where were made, the car inched its way out of the garage. It ground down the gravel driveway and bumped its way through town. As we turned onto the main highway, the road smoothed. The car gained speed and so did the beating of our hearts. We zoomed our way through the twists and turns of Highway 20. We carefully navigated the narrow, sometimes one-way, streets of Nevada City. We searched and searched for the perfect parking place. Finally, all of this accomplished, we trooped our way up to the doors of The Library.

We stood, at attention, barely able to contain our excitement. The ritual we enacted every month was about to enfold. Slowly, my father's hand would reach into his wallet. Slowly, he pulled out his money. Even more slowly, we were each carefully handed a dollar bill. Looking each of us squarely in the eye, with the admonishment to "remember to be quiet—it is still a library," we were set free.

The heavy door pushed open, and we tiptoed inside. The darkened hall greeted us. The smell of books surrounded us. Our eyes darted here and there. Our paths diverged as different titles beckoned. Hands reached, eyes roamed, and each of us was lost in the world of words. Today was the monthly Library Sale. The dollar we had been given was a ticket to a journey to outer space, a ride on a wild stallion through the desert, or lessons on how to knit. So many choices—which option to pick? Should it be four Nancy Drews at twenty-five cents each or one large photography book featuring African animals? Magazines packed a lot of bang for the buck. You could get ten *National Geographics* for one dollar!

We wandered back and forth, around and around, our minds churning. Until, it seemed hours later, choices weighed, decisions made, we proceeded to the checkout desk. There a kindly volunteer greeted us with a warm smile. Reverently, we placed our books on the desk. Pencil in hand, she stared at her receipt book as she added our totals. We hoped that we had calculated correctly, and the dollar was enough to cover our selections. A few times, I think the volunteer creatively added so that my sister's total came in at a dollar. Then the books were respectfully wrapped in paper and handed back to us.

We pushed our way through the heavy doors, blinking in the sunlight, clutching our treasures. Somehow we found our way back to the car. We piled back in, although with less enthusiasm than we had before. The whole process was a bit exhausting. We stared out the windows, lost in the dreams our packages promised. The journey back was something to be endured until we reached home, where we could finally succumb to the spell of the books we had chosen.

Unfortunately, this magic only came once an eon, once a month, at The Library Sale.

Kelly Kolar Valin lives in Nevada City

Linden Tree at Doris Foley Library. *Painting by Tyler Micoleau.*

The Day I Wandered In

BRITTA TIGAN

A PAGE was torn in my only childhood book, *The Color Kittens*. It was the best page—dancing Easter eggs with a magical purple island, pink sea and golden trees. I remember being sad reading the book and coming to that page. Although my parents were well-educated, this Little Golden Book was my only option when I wanted to read.

I was a short and chunky, shy child with four tall, skinny, outgoing siblings. I spent a lot of time alone, paging through my mom's art books, left over from her college years. But photos of the great masters' paintings and awful Currier & Ives prints didn't inspire me. Dad occasionally read *The Rhyme of the Ancient Mariner* to us children. That was torture.

Since my folks weren't readers and we lived on the outskirts of a small Illinois town in the 1950s, I had never been in a library. My small Catholic grade school had no library, and even by age eleven I suspected the texts we read in class.

Our family moved close to town during the summer of 1962, when I was 12 years old. We lived across the street from the library, and I'll never forget the day I wandered into that old brick building. The wonder of it didn't hit me immediately. But when I found a book called *The Pink Dress* and began reading it, I was filled with excitement. Here was a book about a girl my own age, facing many of the same problems. I curled up in a corner and read the book start to finish.

After getting a library card, I checked out *The Hand of Mary Gallico*, a short ghost story. Although I can barely remember many of the thousands books I've read since, those two novels remain clear in my mind. The library became *my place* for life.

I now have a perfect copy of *The Color Kittens* and always read it to my granddaughter Molly when she visits with my son and his wife. And I check out five or so children's books from the Madelyn Helling Library to read with Molly. As I see her eyes light up when she spies the stack of books waiting for her, I know that my love for libraries will continue in my family.

Britta Tigan lives in Nevada City

Those Rows and Rows of Books

MYRNA COURTNEY

I WAS, oh, eight years old or so, living in Antioch, California, and though we had a fun, very old, house with an entertaining flight of stone steps to the street and a handy empty lot next door for playing with neighbor kids, what I remember most was that the library was two blocks away. Walking distance. *Walking distance!* That meant I could go alone, any time I wanted. My mother went with me the first time or two, but she soon tired of running back and forth, sometimes two or three times a day. We would walk up the steps together, push open that heavy door, and there they were. Rows and rows, shelves and shelves of books lining the entire room, floor to ceiling. Just begging to be touched, picked up, thumbed through … and checked out.

I admit to being disappointed when the librarian said I could only check out certain books for my age group, and led me over to a small, three-shelf bookcase. That was it. But still, there were a lot of books stuffed on those shelves. The limit was three at a time, and so I chose three, ran ahead of my mom all the way home, flopped on the screened-in porch and read my way through all of them in a day. It being summer and no school helped.

Back we went for three more. Well, after a few weeks of this, I had read every book on those shelves. I told the librarian. She shrugged and said she was sorry, that's all she had, the rest were too old for me. My heart actually squeezed until I got dizzy. *What are you saying? I can't read any of these books in here?*

I raced out the big door, down the steps and flew home, crying my heart out. I threw myself into my mother's lap and sobbed out my story. Well, she said, rules are rules. *What? WHAT?*

I couldn't believe it and was inconsolable. After a while, my mother said come with me, and together we marched back to the library. Up the steps, in the big door and to the librarian's desk. They talked. I stood behind my mother, not looking at the librarian, not looking at the bookshelves, my heart flip-flopping.

Then my mother leaned over the desk and wrote something on a piece of paper. She smiled and handed it to the librarian, who peered around my mother at me and said, well now. And she wrote out a tiny yellow card with my name on it and handed it to me. There you go, she said.

And my mother said you can read anything you want now. *Anything.*

I was stupefied with joy. Every single book on those shelves was mine for the asking. *Every single one!* Breathing was difficult. Nothing existed for me except that room full of books.

My mother went home and I took my time, running my finger across the titles of every book on all the shelves I could reach. It stopped on a volume of the life of Kit Carson. I took it down and also Buffalo Bill from the same series. And then *Black Beauty* and Nancy Drew and the *Tik Tok of Oz* and a diary of a prairie girl and everything I could find about horses. I couldn't pull books off those shelves fast enough. I lugged the heavy stack to the librarian's desk.

She frowned at the number of books in my arms. But then she looked up at my face and after a thoughtful pause, gave me a big smile. OK, she said, let's get those checked out for you.

I don't remember the walk home.

Myrna Courtney lives in Grass Valley

Home Again

EMMA V. WALL

THE Colusa County Library remains a one-storey cement-block building with a flat roof line. Tall, slim trees and a hedge protect the southeast corner of the façade. As a child, those bushes made me feel that the building was supposed to be concealed. The trees were soldiers standing guard, and the library was a secret, a place meant only for me. One afternoon I hid behind the hedge from my dad, who was just leaving the grocery store across the street. I could hear his voice in my head, *"A dónde vas? Ya hisiste los mandados que te di?"* "Where are you going? Have you run the errands I gave you?" I stayed hidden until he passed; I wanted to visit the library before going home from school.

Every time I entered the library I was immediately comforted by the din of the water fountain and the hum of unknown machines, but mostly I craved the musty paper smell, that warm attic smell that captured and swept me past the front desk and on to the northeast corner, the designated children's section. Usually the blinds were open there. Soft friendly light streamed through the tall windows showing patches of blue sky that cheered me. I hurried to claim my spot by the windows, then looked around to see who else was visiting the library and tried to remain unseen.

I always started there, where I should have been, but as the day wore on, my favorite red bean bag chair and I somehow made our way around the high shelves that formed the barrier to the unknown—the adult section. Unless a librarian found me first, I remained among the grownup books, lying on my side, a leg propped up on the wall. As the years went by the librarians realized I was harmless and left me to my adventure only to kick me out at closing time. And sometimes I didn't even read, but like a cat I'd knead a comfy spot in the bean bag, face toward the tall windows, curl up with a book, and the intent to read, and wind up daydreaming while I watched the trees sway in the breeze.

I knew you weren't supposed to judge a book by its cover, but when I transitioned from picture books to chapter books, since I didn't know any of the authors, the only logical way to *pick* a book was by its cover. If a book's title, cover, jacket information or even its shape caught my attention, I added that book to the pile on the bean bag that followed me from section to section. In this way *The Valley of the Dolls,* which I imagined must be about a magical place where dolls came to life, ended up on the bean bag next to me. I soon learned the "dolls" were pills and adults weren't all they were cracked up to be, which did surprise me, but I never stopped hoping for the main character, a real doll, to enter the story.

Out in front, in plain sight, some people worked at the long wooden tables. I only did that when I was older and only when my friends and I did homework. Once, when I was 13, as I sat at one of those very tables in an uncomfortable, straight-backed wooden chair, I got a call from Dad, telling me to come home because it was dark. *"Hija ya es tarde, ya vengase."* My friends giggled, then snickered. My dad's booming voice could be heard clear to the front desk. The librarian held her index finger in front of her pursed lips making a soft "shushing" sound. I looked at her helplessly.

In my room at home I had a plain brown Formica table; this was my desk and the one place I had to display my few books. Next to the desk I hung a "Books I've Read" list. It stretched from the ceiling to the floor and more than halfway down again. When I read the list, which I did over and over, I could see not only the cover of each book, but also the exact place it was shelved in the library. This connection gave me a great sense of accomplishment, peace, and, utter happiness. I was home again.

Emma V. Wall lives in Rocklin

Treasure Hunting

ELIZABETH UNRUH

THIS world has always been full of treasure hunters, searching for the one thing they value above all else: gold, priceless gems, or Spanish doubloons. But not all treasure chests are filled with material wealth. For some, the treasure is found in books. Some of my earliest memories are of clutching my mother's hand as we climbed what seemed like a countless number of stairs to the door of our small community library. Once inside I would hurry softly to the children's section and look through the colorful selection of books, pulling out the ones that caught my attention for a closer inspection. After gathering the books of my choice and locating my mom, we made our way over to the checkout counter. If I stood on my tiptoes I could just see over the counter so I could watch as the librarian went through the same routine of scanning the book, placing the little yellow card with the return date into the pocket inside the cover, and finally stacking them together in a neat little pile. Lastly, she would scan my mom's white library card, the key to the treasure. With our arms laden we would say our goodbyes and leave our little library until the next visit.

Another treasured memory is that momentous day when at five I had mastered the ability to write my first and last name, and so was able to receive my own library card. I remember being handed the blue card, upon which I painstakingly printed my name, and then it was mine; my very own key to the treasure. From that day forth I could proudly hand the librarian my own card when I checked out books, knowing it was my responsibility to take care of the books and return them on time.

As I grew, so did my love of books, and with the wealth of the library at my fingertips I could explore the world of literature to my heart's content. Rising up through the ranks, I graduated from the whimsical rhyming tales of Dr. Seuss into the exciting adventures of Pippi Longstocking and Mrs. Piggle-Wiggle, finally delving into the great masterpieces of *The Great Gatsby*, *A Tale of Two Cities*, *Wuthering Heights*, and *Tess of the D'Urbervilles*. My mom was always the key figure in feeding my passion for reading, forever giving me new and exciting books to devour. Whenever I found myself lacking in literature she would come to my rescue, her arms embracing books for me to choose from.

Every book has its own personality, a history of its very own. I love purchasing old books; their covers worn and soft with time and handling, the slightly yellowing pages, and that wonderful bookish smell of paper, ink, and dust.

Another thing I always look for is an inscription or name inside the cover; little messages indicating the occasion for which the book was given. Books are a wonderful treasure, not meant to be buried and hidden away, but shared, discussed and enjoyed. The library is a doorway to adventure, mystery, romance, history, comedy, tragedy, and so many other things. It is a treasure chest. All we have to do is turn the key, lift the lid, and commandeer its bounty.

Elizabeth Unruh, age 16, lives in Grass Valley

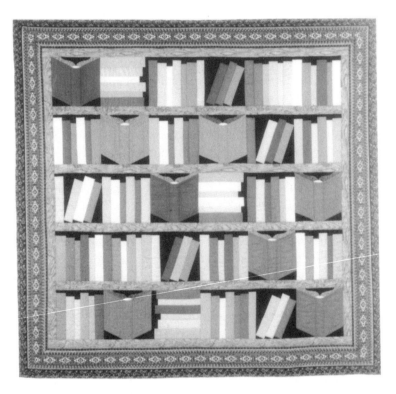

Library Quilt. *Designed and quilted by Ruth Heyser, Library Assistant at the Josiah Royce Branch Library in Grass Valley.*

Too Much Reading

RUBY TOTTEN

WOODRUFF Memorial Library in La Junta, Colorado, was an imperial white stone edifice so intimidating to this six-year-old that, if it hadn't been for the humble back door to the children's department I may never have summoned the courage to fill out a card. As it was, I was almost grown before I crept up the outside stone steps to the front entrance and went through those filigreed, corbelled and pillared portals.

But through that back wooden door I went countless times and, today at 82 I can still summon up the wondrous magical feeling of standing inside and knowing I had access to every book within eyesight.

Getting to the library was not without its risks. It was about eight blocks from home, and in one stretch there was a boy my age who felt compelled to throw rocks at me, and in another a fierce dog that never left his yard, but bared his teeth at me for the length of his property. I had to run this gauntlet coming and going. I persevered, however. Those trips were vital.

Then, as time went by, I incurred my mom's displeasure by reading *too much*. She forbade the library trips, feeling I should be outside more, instead of collapsed into a huge overstuffed chair. It was too late. Books had become as essential as air to me. I continued the trips and found hiding places for the books at home. But I neglected to get the books back on time, ran up charges, and couldn't pay them. Eventually desperation and booklessness forced me to admit my guilt. My parents' disapproval was thunderous. However, after requiring me to earn my own fee, they admitted defeat and let me return to my beloved Woodruff Memorial. Another of the feelings I can readily summon up today is the exhilaration I felt that day, plopping the overdue penalty on the librarian's desk, free once again to wander among the shelves.

Throughout my life, libraries have had enormous impact ranging from an introduction to rarefied ideas to preparing me for earning a living. Reading on an enormous variety of subjects enabled me as an adult to take on a career in journalism that I enjoyed for the next quarter century.

Ruby Totten is a Book Buddy for the Friends of the Nevada County Library, and is a caregiver for one of the oldest cats in Nevada County

Sting

DONNA HANELIN

THE only time I remember being bored as a child was at my cousin Beth's house playing a game of our own device called "Library." Our mothers sat just around the corner at the kitchen table; Library (the game) allowed us the comfort of their voices while we played. We were both bookish and most happy at the public library, lost in story and dream. Nonetheless, playing Library didn't prove to have a lot of thrills in it. I longed to be back with my neighbor boy, sitting on top of the wall between our houses, stoning the lions who snarled at our feet, but this was not to be—our mothers were drinking coffee, eating pastry, talking and talking.

I sat at the desk while Beth slowly chose four books. When she brought them to me, I opened up the back of each one and stuck in a piece of paper scribbled with a pretend-date two weeks away. Two weeks three days later, she returned the books. "Your books are overdue." I used my most serious voice.

She blushed. She was sorry, but it didn't matter. Three cents a day for each overdue book. Then it was her turn to be the librarian. I chose three books.

"Only three?"

"They're fat ones," I said. When I brought them back before two weeks, she tried to act surprised.

The game hobbled on until Mom suggested we go outside since it was such a nice spring day and we didn't want to stay inside (did we?) when the sun was shining. Beth did want to stay inside, but I was heading out the back door halfway through my mother's declarative question. The grass looked so cool and soft I took off my shoes and went skipping through the clover-spotted lawn. One of those step-hops landed me on a honey bee, at which point the whole day came into sharp and vital focus. I had never been stung by a bee before, and found it much more riveting than "Library."

Fifteen years after that bee sting I had the good fortune of landing a work-study job at the San Francisco Art Institute as a librarian's assistant. Harry, a real librarian, was my boss. It was a small library but most of the books were gorgeous, oversized art ones—even shelving them was fun; first checking that Harry was safely inside his glass cubicle, I often flipped through not only the book I was shelving, but also several of its neighbors. After Harry taught me how to do simple book repairs, I checked each checked-in book for tears and breaks, incidentally luxuriating in every full color picture. What a job!

That summer I was still employed at the library; on the weekends, Jim (my fiancé) and I fled the city with our new canvas tent and green, rattling Coleman stove. Before this particular trip I had noticed on our map an area covered with blue puddles. "Let's go here," I shouted down the hall to Jim, "It has lots of lakes, all close together!" I was pointing to Gold Lake Road off Highway 49, just a couple hours drive from my present home in Nevada City.

For two glorious days Jim and I hiked and swam, breathing in the brightest and clearest air I had ever known. The lakes were bracingly cold, but each more picture-perfect than the last and once back on the trail it didn't take long to heat up again, primed for the next plunge. I had never been so happy in all my life: marriage on the horizon, art school, a library job, the sparkling air and waters of the Sierra Nevada.

"Let's stay another day," I said to Jim.

"But don't you have to be at the library on Tuesday?"

"I'll call Harry in the morning. I'll just tell him I've never been so happy in all my life and I'd like to stay another day."

"Maybe you should tell him you're sick," Jim said. "A lot of people don't want to go back to work because they're happier away from work."

I didn't understand Jim's logic. I thought my happiness extremely important, and surely the rest of the world would concur; so I called Harry and I didn't lie. I told him I had never been so happy. He told me I had to be at work on Tuesday or I wouldn't have a job.

I was stung. "Sure Harry, I'll be there ... yes ... no, I feel fine ... sure, tomorrow ... bye."

As Jim and I broke camp, I felt heavy-hearted and, regrettably, a little more grown-up. I went back to the city and continued checking books in and out for another semester—even now, when on a whim I drive up Highway 49 to the place I was once the happiest, the image comes double-exposed with stacks of art books waiting to be shelved, piled on the sandy floor of a clear mountain lake.

Donna Hanelin is a writer and a teacher living in Nevada City

What We Remember
DALE PENDELL

Someday all the books will be gone—
the libraries burned, rotted with mildew,
or sunk into the earth from their own
accumulated weight—missed only
by a few scholars: "Would that we could find
another fragment ... Sappho, Arkilochus."

Freed from texts, beguiled nonetheless
by our own hallucinations, new myths
setting the wet clay of memory:
crickets, sandhill cranes, or
alpine volcanoes, snow—covered, above
a pristine fjord—women's bodies uplifting
the soft Sonoma hills.

A thousand feet of silt has flattened
the Valley. Just what is: the only
language left to us now. Or
"Once, long ago ..."
     the fire burns low.
A coyote might howl, if we
are lucky. That you and I
found no way to build a world
atop the destruction of the old one—
to hear the song that Turtle sings, earless,
when the moon is darkest, that ...

Thus the hills return to valleys—
sand pipers, vast tidelands—
awaiting the new mountains
of an icy, distant eon:
cranes, or geese, a glyph—
crickets, a cool summer, the elk
returned, grizzlies, wolves—
whatever is left
when we are finally
done with our dreaming.

Dale Pendell from Penn Valley is the author of the Pharmako Trilogy *and, most recently,* Inspired Madness: the Gift of Burning Man

The Libraries at Ephesus, at Alexandria

C. B. FOLLETT

In the photo, my mother
sits in a black beret and striped dress,
one of seven on a bench with masts
in the background. Lots of hats,
men in shirts and white flannels behind them.
The sun is hot, no wind stirs their sleeves.
My father stands behind my mother,
his hand on her shoulder.
There's no writing on the back
so I don't know the others, or the year.

Why do I have this one picture
from all the albums I used to look through
searching for my father? Albums
I would have saved and pored over.

But Mother threw them out,
I knew no one would want them.

I thought of the great libraries of Ephesus,
of Alexandria,
burned to the ground
in ancient times:
lost learning,
lost past.

*C. B. Follett, a poet and the publisher
of Arctos Press, lives in Sausalito*

I Was a Feral Child Raised by Republicans

RICHARD STOCKTON

I WAS a feral child raised by Republicans. I can picture my mother wearing her "I Like Ike" button on her apron after the '56 election, "He is a saint for fighting for our freedom." Why did I go organic after such a white bread beginning? How did I become a "free spirit" instead of a "reasonably priced spirit?" Where did I get these friends who chant "We are all one," when my first family's prayer was, "We are all looking out for number one?" What made me get into "I search for adventure" instead of "I search for tax breaks?"

It happened at the library. From eight years of age I would curl up on creaky oak chairs and let the pages transform me into characters pursuing high, scandalous adventure. The beautiful thing about my escape was that nobody knew I was gone. Or where I went. Nobody knew I traveled mean streets with Sam Spade, traveled the seamy side of Hollywood with Sammy Glick. Nobody knew when I learned that "proletariat" was neither a type of cheese or a racehorse. Nobody knew when I learned that Karl Marx was not Groucho's dad. Nobody guessed that the skinny kid with the baseball glove under his chair was inhabiting the bodies of exciting, quixotic people. In the library I learned, "You can be someone, or you can be someone else." The library set me free.

Now, forty-five years later I'm hearing, "To protect our freedoms we have to give up some," and hearing Attorney General John Ashcroft say that "any American who questions The Patriot Act is a terrorist," and that The Homeland Security Department can go into libraries and demand anyone's reading records. Excuse me? So what if I've checked out sixteen books on cross-dressing, is this the kind of thing I want other people to know about?

I must test the system.

I'm in Santa Cruz, California, producing a comedy show for Comcast Television, and with my hair bureaucratically short and my double-breasted suit intimidating, I'm ready for the test. I use all my method-acting techniques to make myself become "Mark Miller, Homeland Security." I eat at Denny's and rearrange the jelly packets by flavor. As I walk towards the library I whip out a camera and photograph cars that have peace symbols. I listen for conversations that should be in "Free Speech Zones."

As I enter the Santa Cruz Library I think no one is at the desk. Then I look down and see a tiny woman who gazes up with the confidence of someone who knows she has bumped her head far less than me. Her glasses make her eyes look so big she could be an Anime character. She is patient.

"My name is Mark Miller and . . . ," I lean towards her, "I work for The Homeland Security Department." Her back arches, her eyes glaze and she sucks in her breath and holds it.

"We have a list of titles and we'd like to know who is checking these books out, so I need access to your files about who is reading these books."

The muscles in her jaw bulge, her right temple twitches, her chest heaves, her lips turn white from compression. She lifts one foot, slams it down and crosses her arms over her chest.

I whisper, "Look, we don't want any trouble here."

She does not budge. We are eyeball to eyeball, unblinking. I can feel my contact lenses drying out. We are locked together, balancing on the edge of a legal razor.

The deafening silence between us makes people look. A round laughing face bounces in between us and shouts, "You're the comedian ... the guy who interviews people on Channel Four!" My cover is blown, I'm busted, it's over. The tiny woman relaxes slowly, a cautious smile comes to her mouth, and then she laughs.

As I look at this woman who would not back down from the Federal Government, who would face imprisonment to protect her library, my mother's words about Eisenhower come back, "He is a saint for fighting for our freedom." I think, "OK Mom, but a saint is also someone who will go to jail for our freedom."

Richard Stockton of Cedar Ridge is a stand-up comic and author of Fondle the Fear

Close to Heaven

GINA GIPPNER

WHEN I was in the seventh grade I had an angry heart and a wild spirit that needed to be tamed. It didn't seem to matter where I was or who I was with, I could find trouble in the blink of an eye. One day I decided I would be fashionably late to class, and as I walked into the classroom I heard, "Gina, I want you to take this hall pass and head to the library. I want you to find a dictionary and write the definitions of 50 words. When you are finished you may come back to the class and share with us your favorite word!" I can still see my teacher handing me the hall pass, and when she did she was smiling. I believe with all my heart she was praying for me, and that God had shared with her a place where I would find the comfort I was seeking. I was seeking others who knew exactly what I was feeling and I found them the moment I opened the library door.

That day marked the beginning of my new-found friends. I was introduced to a man called Jesus when I pulled an ol' Bible off the shelf. I was introduced to a man named Mark Twain. He wrote about two boys that were always getting into trouble. I met a woman named Margaret Mitchell who wrote about a young girl named, Miss Scarlett. I loved the way Miss Scarlett would think about things "tomorrow." She didn't seem to let her failures occupy her "today!" And then I met a woman named Louisa May Alcott. Her book titled *Little Women* remains my favorite. She was able to define me in her character Jo. I was born an aspiring writer and didn't know it until I was well into my 30s.

I believe with all my heart that the library is the closest place to heaven I will ever be. There is silence where I'm able to disappear into my thoughts while reading of those who "thought" before me. There is freedom in reading of those who fought before me so I could have the "freedom" to read, and I love the simplicity of a library. The moment I open a library door I am reminded of a teacher who cared enough to share with me the importance of words. The only definition I brought back to her that day read as follows: "My *American Heritage Dictionary* defines the word library as: A place in which literary and artistic materials, such as books, periodicals, newspapers, and recordings are kept for reading, reference or lending."

I don't believe there is a kinder word.

Gina Gippner lives in Penn Valley

Lost and Gone Forever

CHERYL KLEIN

ONE of my earliest library memories also happens to be one of my few memories of childhood disobedience. My mom had been a children's librarian before taking time off to raise my sister and me, so the three of us spent many hours at the Manhattan Beach Public Library. Cathy and I pulled kid-sized wire chairs up to a giant, shag-carpeted, table-like mound in the children's section while my mom browsed the new arrivals.

My favorite book, which I checked out over and over again, was a picture book illustrating the song "Clementine." (You know—"Oh my darling, oh my darling, oh my daaaarling Clementine . . . .") A quick Amazon search doesn't bring up anything resembling my memories of '70s-style green, orange, and brown illustrations of the lost Clementine and her distraught miner-forty-niner father, so I suspect it's out of print. I'm sure a quick call to the research desk could tell me a lot more than Amazon though.

I think it was the setting and the mystery of the Clementine story that appealed to me: I pictured the cavern and the canyon of the song as desolate places full of dark, intriguing corners. Then there was the tragic heroine with her ruby-lips-above-the-water, the covered wagon rattling toward the river and arriving too late, the fact that the "splinter" that sent her careening into the foaming brine was in fact *gold!*

This book was the first in a long line of Western narratives I would fall in love with, from *Little House on the Prairie* to Cynthia Kadohata's futuristic, dystopic Los Angeles in *In the Heart of the Valley of Love.* In kindergarten, I would wear a bonnet to school. In college I would drive through Hollywood marveling at lost and tragic locals. In my mid-20s I would write my own novel about a girl lost in a mine long ago, and a contemporary girl obsessed with finding out what happened to her.

But first I would do the unthinkable (at least for a librarian's daughter): I would draw in a library book.

I must have been about four. There must have been a blue ballpoint pen nearby. There was a lot of white space on some of the Clementine book's pages, and it seemed too white, somehow. I uncapped the pen and drew several tiny blue squares. Maybe a triangle or two.

I was an obsessively well-behaved child, so it wasn't about transgression. Rather, I liked the idea of adding my own contribution to an existing story that I loved. If there were missing parts, I wanted to fill them. If I could thicken or twist the mystery a little bit, even better.

Eventually I was led by the hand to the tall Formica counter top of the circulation desk. I probably apologized. I don't know if my mom had to pay for the book, but I know I didn't get to take it home with me again. It disappeared into library ether.

It's funny—I don't own copies of most of my favorite books. An out-of-print Lynda Barry comic book graduated with my sophomore-year dorm resident advisor. An ex-roommate's ex-boyfriend has my copy of *The Hours*. Michelle Tea's *The Chelsea Whistle* could be in the hands of any number of people I raved to about that book. I don't mind, though—I like being a library.

Libraries taught me to be a thief (while I always return what I borrow from the LAPL, I swear!—I do have a thick stack of books "borrowed" indefinitely from friends), a foolishly generous lender, and most importantly, a graffiti artist: As readers we are born into a vast expanse of stories, and as writers, it's our job to paint over them in the most respectful way possible.

Cheryl Klein directs the California office of Poets & Writers, Inc.; her collection of connected stories, The Commuters, *won City Works Press' Ben Reitman Award*

Luddite in the Library

JUDIE RAE

MY association with the library began early; I recall sitting on a minuscule chair in the children's section listening, enamored, while a librarian read to her charges *Mrs. Piggle Wiggle*. Mrs. Piggle Wiggle was a tiny bit of a woman who lived alone in an upside-down house. I was both enchanted and mystified as to how one navigated upside-down stairs; indeed, this dilemma kept me occupied for quite some time. (To this one small incident I credit my inability to visualize math problems. But give me a misplaced modifier any day.)

As I recall, Mrs. Piggle Wiggle had no visible means of support (no occupation, no husband), though I think she was once married to a pirate. (One wonders if he lived in Washington D.C.) Mrs. Piggle Wiggle was always on call to help frustrated parents solve difficulties with their children. For the youngster who refused to eat, Mrs. Piggle Wiggle had a set of graduated dishes, the smallest of which held a teaspoon of food and a thimbleful of liquid. By the time the prepubescent ingrate had finished using all the dishes, he was not only starving but also quite weak. That's when Mrs. Piggle Wiggle went into action, organizing a children's parade in which the hunger-strike victim could not participate. She also had a parrot that talked back and rivaled any obnoxious child. You had a creepy kid, she had a cure.

Mrs. Piggle Wiggle was my kind of woman.

As a student in junior high, I marched into the library, alone, and waded through books in order to write a paper on Greek columns. Today I could no longer tell you the difference between an Ionic and a Doric column, and one might question the need to hold such information in one's head, but the point is that at thirteen or so, I learned that knowledge was there for the gleaning, and it was gleaned in the library.

In high school my boyfriend worked in the library, shelving books. The librarian at the time was all of thirty, though to me she seemed incredibly old and bent on ruining my romance. She wore sensible shoes and Peter Pan collars, and she was always shushing me and suggesting I leave the premises, as Richard could not shelve and talk at the same time. (As it was a small library with few aisles of books, I was limited as to hiding places and was usually forced to leave or to pretend interest in my homework, which in those days, took a back seat to love.)

Fast forward a few years to my epiphany of sorts, which occurred in the Malibu Branch of the Los Angeles County Library. It was there, during a thunderstorm, that the electricity went out and the computers went down. This was a time of transition for the County and they still had the card catalogs. "Ah ha!" I thought. Card catalogs do not lose electricity. It was the beginning of my life as a Luddite, rejecting progress when at all possible. Give me a card catalog any day. (Now if only I could find one!)

Today my relationship with the library has come full circle and I find myself taking my granddaughter to story time and to check out books. She's still too young for *Mrs. Piggle Wiggle*, though I hope one day to introduce her to this treasure from my childhood. Aubrey's idea of a good read is *Pigs in the Mud in the Middle of the Rud*. This well-worn charmer has been perused and studied many times by a three-year-old, who already knows what it means to love a book.

This is the Luddite speaking, but it saddens me that so many students today use the Internet exclusively and will never know the wonder of the touch and scent of books, or the serendipitous experience of finding willy nilly just what they were looking for amongst the stacks. Will they ever know the delicious feel of entering the library on a cold day, finding within its walls a comforting place of refuge?

My job as college English instructor allows me to mandate that students acquaint themselves with the inside of an institution which has served so many of us so well for so long. I worry, though, that the books that have sustained us through a lifetime could become obsolete in a society not disposed to honoring artistic endeavors. It is for those of us who love books to ensure that libraries exist for generations to come.

Judie Rae teaches writing at Sierra College and is the author of many articles and books, including a Nancy Drew mystery

The Library Is Dead

DAVID FENIMORE

MY employer, The University of Nevada at Reno, is building a new "library." That's what we call it, my fellow faculty members and our students. However, our official website calls it a "knowledge center." It will be "a centralized seamless bridge to a wide variety of digital media such as graphics, audio, video, and print." Only 20% of the books will be located on the familiar shelves, the rest retrievable only by some monstrous claw that will deliver them, I presume, to a circulation desk resembling the bridge of the Starship *Enterprise*.

At first, like many of us, I threw up my hands in horror. What, no browsing the stacks? I come from Philadelphia, where Benjamin Franklin and friends pooled their precious leather-bound volumes to create the first public library. Centuries later, a bookish boy could wander the aisles of his suburban branch, finding a freedom and diversity denied him at home or school. I discovered science fiction, and checked out armloads to fuel my summer reveries. After college I escaped to the West, because its mountains and deserts were the closest I'd ever get to Mars. I still approach this world, and my classrooms, with something of that wide-eyed wonder.

I loved those dusty bookshelves and reading tables, but libraries are living things, not monuments or museums. Even then I found my youthful interests outstripping mere print: I scanned old magazines on microfilm, turned the pages of giant map atlases, listened to Stravinsky and Sinatra records, and learned to thread the projector with 16mm footage of early rocket launches and a Ray Bradbury documentary that made me think of becoming a writer. My library was indeed a "seamless bridge."

Franklin's heirs know they must centralize new ways of transmitting knowledge so today's kids can daydream like I did. Books work—their weatherproof portability, long storage life, high-contrast screens and easy browse features are hard to beat. Once they were even considered newfangled: Plato says Socrates complained that writing would destroy the minds of the younger generation. So I am wary of the old professor's prejudice that books are better for you than images and hypertext. The photographs of Jacob Riis and Dorothea Lange stirred more compassion for human misery than a thousand indignant essays could muster; ditto the movie *The Grapes of Wrath* and the acorn.org website.

Another boy's life: In 1930, after a bored Woody Guthrie dropped out of school, he began haunting the Pampa, Texas, public library. He read history, world literature, Eastern mysticism—"every kind of an 'ology,' 'osis,' 'itis,' and 'ism' there was," he said, and typed reports for librarian Evelyn Todd. He wrote his own psychology textbook, which she catalogued. By the 1940s he was an artist, a musician, a communist, and a compulsive writer. He spent nights at a borrowed typewriter, banging away at 150 words per minute about everything he saw, heard or thought—conversations, current events, politics, poetry, lyrics, jokes and assorted folk wisdom. Friends would find him asleep the next morning under dozens of pages, some of which turned into songs, radical newspaper columns, and his fictionalized autobiography *Bound for Glory,* its vernacular voice an influence on Jack Kerouac (himself a speed typist), Bob Dylan, and other Sixties shapers.

Woody's high-velocity keyboarding propelled him beyond books to create exuberant new forms based on oral traditions. Every library patron, young or old, has this chance to access the past, explore the present and create new futures, which today means web pages, databases, e-books, movies, maps, blogs and podcasts, what Allen Ginsberg once called "private literature that goes 1400 miles an hour." Donna Harraway calls us all "cyborgs," our biological beings woven into machines, dependent on automobiles, lightbulbs, phones, laptops and earbuds. Woody, I like to think, was part typewriter, subversively engaged in Harraway's "technostrategic discourse."

It can be hard to learn new tricks. "That's not writing, that's typing," Truman Capote sneered at *On the Road.* I hear some of my colleagues protesting the new media, and avoiding it in their classrooms. I say, don't worry—books aren't going away. You can read them by candlelight, and you can take them backpacking. But they are no longer quite so central to the storage and retrieval of civilization. I read books in an armchair, but I also work on a laptop in the library lobby, browsing DVDs, downloading text, editing images, and embedding music into multimedia presentations I post on my course website.

Thanks to our new Knowledge Center, many of my students will do these same things. The library is dead; long live the library!

David Fenimore lives at North Lake Tahoe and teaches English and Core Humanities at the University of Nevada, Reno; he's still thinking about buying an iPod

Afterword

RAY BRADBURY

I DIDN'T know it, but I was literally writing a dime novel. In the spring of 1950 it cost me nine dollars and eighty cents in dimes to write and finish the first draft of *The Fire Man,* which later became *Fahrenheit 451.*

In all the years from 1941 to that time, I had done most of my typing in the family garages, either in Venice, California (where we lived because we were poor, not because *it* was the "in" place to be) or behind the tract house where my wife, Marguerite, and I raised our family. I was driven out of my garage by my loving children, who insisted on coming around to the rear window and singing and tapping on the panes. Father had to choose between finishing a story or playing with the girls. I chose to play, of course, which endangered the family income. An office had to be found. We couldn't afford one.

Finally, I located just the place, the typing room in the basement of the library at the University of California at Los Angeles. There, in neat rows, were a score or more of old Remington or Underwood typewriters which rented out at a dime a half hour. You thrust your dime in, the clock ticked madly, and you typed wildly, to finish before the half hour ran out. Thus I was twice driven; by children to leave home, and by a typewriter timing device to be a maniac at the keys. Time was indeed money. I finished the first draft in roughly nine days. At 25,000 words, it was half the novel it eventually would become.

Between investing dimes and going insane when the typewriter jammed (for there went your precious time!) and whipping pages in and out of the device, I wandered upstairs. There I strolled, lost in love, down the corridors, and through the stacks, touching books, pulling volumes out, turning pages, thrusting volumes back, drowning in all the good stuffs that are the essence of libraries. What a place, don't you agree, to write a novel about burning books in the Future!

So much for pasts. What about *Fahrenheit 451* in this day and age. Have I changed my mind about much that it said to me, when I was a younger writer? Only if by change you mean has my love of libraries widened and deepened, to which the answer is a yes that ricochets off the stacks and dusts talcum off the librarian's cheek. Since writing this book, I have spun more stories, novels, essays, and poems about writers than any other writer in history that I can think of. I have written poems about Melville, Melville and Emily Dickinson, Emily Dickinson and Charles Dickens, Hawthorne, Poe, Edgar Rice Burroughs, and along the way I compared Jules Verne and his Mad Captain to Melville and his equally obsessed mariner. I have scribbled poems about librarians, taken night trains with my favorite authors across the continental wilderness, staying up all night gambling and drinking, drinking and chatting. I warned Melville, in one poem, to stay away from land (it never was his stuff!) and turned Bernard Shaw into a robot, so as to conveniently stow him aboard a rocket and wake him on the long journey to Alpha Centaun to hear his Prefaces piped off his tongue and into my delighted ear. I have written a Time Machine story in which I hum back to sit at the deathbeds of Wilde, Melville, and Poe to tell of my love and warm their bodies in their last hours. . . . But, enough. As you can see, I am madness maddened when it comes to "books, writers, and the great granary silos where their wits are stored."

Ray Bradbury, one of America's great writers, lives in Southern California; excerpted from the Afterword of Farenheit 451

Ray Bradbury.

Nevada County Library Foundation

The Nevada County Library Foundation was established in 1997 to provide private support for the county libraries. It receives, manages, and disburses funds from gifts and bequests. Your gift or bequest, regardless of size, makes it possible for the Nevada County Library to sustain a level of excellence and to expand resources, programs, public services, and facilities. Donations in any amount are welcome. We are particularly grateful to the Foundation for supporting *Open to All*.

Friends of the Nevada County Libraries

The mission of the Friends of Nevada County Libraries, a nonprofit organization, is to focus community attention on the continuing value of, and necessity for, a public library system as a cultural, educational, and recreational asset. In order to carry out that purpose the Friends seek out gifts of materials, service, and money; raise funds for the purchase of library materials and furnishings; collect and resell previously-owned books; and sponsor many educational and recreational library programs.

Friends of the Truckee Library

Established in 1971, the Friends is an independent organization that supports our Truckee Library. The Friends sponsor cultural community events such as poetry readings, publishing workshops, year-round book sales, and "Truckee Reads," a town-wide reading project with a weekend of book discussions and programs. The Friends promote and support the Library's offerings for children, such as the Winter and Summer Reading Programs. The Friends raise money throughout the year to fund these and other projects for the Truckee Library.

To donate to any of the above worthy organizations and find out more about library services, please visit the library website at
www.mynevadacounty.com/library